*The Smaller
Liberal Arts College*

THE LIBRARY OF EDUCATION

A Project of The Center for Applied Research in Education, Inc.

Categories of Coverage

I	II	III
Curriculum and Teaching	Administration, Organization, and Finance	Psychology for Educators

IV	V	VI
History, Philosophy, and Social Foundations	Professional Skills	Educational Institutions

The Smaller Liberal Arts College

LEWIS B. MAYHEW

School of Education
Stanford University

The Center for Applied Research in Education, Inc.
New York

Second printing.......September, 1965

LIBRARY OF CONGRESS
CATALOG CARD NO.: 62–18289

PRINTED IN THE UNITED STATES OF AMERICA

Foreword

It is inevitable that colleges and universities should occupy an ambivalent place in society even though society creates, supports, and at times praises them. The fact of the matter is that what really goes on within collegiate halls is not generally understood.

I have long assumed that this misunderstanding is a necessary by-product of the paradoxical ends for which these institutions exist. A college is established by society to insure that the values to which the society subscribes are perpetuated; there is, in effect, an orthodoxy at stake. And yet, in its rarer moments society acknowledges that it is equally important to examine and, indeed, modify that orthodoxy. Thus the college is mandated to question the value system which it is also supposed to preserve. A problem arises, however, from the fact that the whole society does not uniformly subscribe to both these ends. There are always some to whom it appears that the college ought to be preserving instead of questioning. And to others the reverse is true. This is why colleges are so often misunderstood by the society which sustains them.

While I am not ready to abandon this explanation, Dr. Mayhew's book has forced me to think it through again, for what he suggests is that our problem is essentially one of our own making. Put bluntly, it is a question of being misunderstood, not simply because we do not explain ourselves well to those outside, but because we cannot even explain ourselves to ourselves.

Oddly enough it is the institution here examined—the liberal arts college—which has most persistently demanded that its sister institutions get on with the job of defending what it considers to be their aberrations. It has taken a somewhat pious stance in this matter, assuming rather archly that if the waters have been muddied over time they have been stirred by the comparative late-comers, the large comprehensive universities, the professional colleges, and, of course, the two-year community colleges. Polishing its label, the liberal arts college has not often seen fit to join in the effort, for, after all, its roots go deep, if not to the Greek academy at least to the "artes liberales" of the medieval university. If you question this, you are summarily referred to the introductory paragraphs of the college catalogue, but I would warn you to read only the introduction. The course listings which follow tend to dissipate the effect.

But Dr. Mayhew read on and, more than this, he discussed his growing dismay with a good many of the people who were responsible for the later sections. He did this, the reader will discover, with a genuine and affectionate concern for what has been happening to an institution which, if true to its purposes, has as much to offer us in the future as it has offered us in the past. It is a concern, by the way, which especially in these troubled times all of us should share.

It would appear that since we have come this far, it may be time to admit that the term "liberal arts" has been emptied of much of its meaning. I rather hate to concede this for I am reluctant to see the tradition of which we speak deprived of its relevance and discarded. The point is that it has relevance, if only we will rediscover it.

It has become obvious that the close relationship we expect to find between the ideals of liberal education and its practice has been strained. It would appear that many of these colleges are no longer faithful to the tradition they espouse. Indeed, the major contribution of Dr. Mayhew's book may be to show the liberal arts college that its primary problem lies in the fact that the first glowing paragraphs of its catalogue have been dimmed by much that follows, that, in other words, there *is* a difference between what it is and what it tells the world it is. He suggests that only when this is recognized will it be possible to overcome many of the difficulties which currently beset it.

This Socratic admonition to know thyself has, of course, been overlooked by more segments of higher education than I care to admit in a budget hearing. But this book, fortunately, is concerned with the small liberal arts college. Those of us connected with complex university systems have been given a dispensation, by omission, which we do not really deserve.

Dr. Mayhew's book succeeds in asking the right questions and in putting together answers which warrant our attention. This does not mean that they will be enthusiastically endorsed by all. Anyone who has long been concerned with higher education has ideas (for the most part, fiercely held) about the value of institutional smallness, of faculty responsibility for the curriculum, about the nature and limitations of student counselling, about what administrations should and should not do. We have all been tempted to write our own books on these questions, but few of us have.

It seems exceedingly odd that our institutions of higher learning have for so many years escaped the careful analysis which other social institutions have received. I am not here referring, of course, to studies of administrative procedures or resource manipulation. These continue to be made, and while some are unquestionably useful I would not like to suggest the notion that all of our problems can be solved by increasing their volume. On the contrary, what is noticeably lacking is a careful reassessment of the very nature of higher learning and how well or badly that nature is being expressed by the institutional forms we have developed. That we have seen so little of this is particularly baffling when we recall that it is in our colleges that many of our best, most curious, and critical minds are to be found.

But this may be changing. Dr. Mayhew's book is but one of an increasing number now appearing which try to get at the problem. Perhaps some day we shall know as much about our colleges and universities as we now know about corporations, political parties, and teen-age gangs. And this would be helpful.

THOMAS H. HAMILTON
President
State University of New York

Contents

CHAPTER I

The Liberal Arts College and Changing
    Times   1

CHAPTER II

The Faculty: Problem or Potential   17

CHAPTER III

The Curriculum: Visions and Distortions   36

CHAPTER IV

Student Personnel: Problems of Balance   54

CHAPTER V

Administration: Leadership or Laissez-
    Faire   74

CHAPTER VI

Finances: Ever-Present Problem   93

Bibliography   106

Index   109

The Smaller
Liberal Arts College

CHAPTER I

The Liberal Arts College
and Changing Times

For half a century it has been predicted that the privately supported liberal arts college would soon disappear from the American educational scene. Yet the four-year liberal arts college, rooted in American civilization, continues to exist and to educate an appreciable percentage of students seeking higher education. In spite of severe limitations in finances, personnel, and physical facilities, the privately supported liberal arts college attracts students and, judging by the subsequent educational and professional achievements of its graduates, does an effective job of educating a good many of them.

While four-year liberal arts colleges differ markedly, they have many characteristics in common, and even their differences fall within a pattern applicable to most. Perhaps the limits of this pattern may best be shown by describing several institutions which demonstrate some of the needs they continue to satisfy and some of the different ways in which they are meeting these needs.

Institution A is an independent Christian college in an industrial and metropolitan area. Originally established as a seminary, it was later converted into a four-year liberal arts college supported by a Southern branch of a Protestant church and located in a small community in a rural area. Then the hardships of the depression years, a change in the composition of the religious group supporting the institution, and the invitation of interested city people led the governing board to move the college to the metropolitan region where it is now situated. As a college supported by a religious group, the institution had sought to provide a liberal education for the youth of the denomination and to prepare teachers for the public schools and religious workers for the denomination. But once it moved, it attempted to do these same things for a larger constituency and to provide a variety of new services. It offered evening courses for

1

adults, maintained an extension service for a large geographical area, provided vocational training for young people who would be absorbed by the local industries, and grew into one of the major cultural centers of the new community. To make it possible for the college to accomplish such purposes, the community supplied considerable financial support which permitted expansion of the faculty and eventually construction of a large multipurpose building to house the principal operations of the school.

The institution is always busy, with classes beginning early in the morning and continuing late into the night. It offers 465 courses ranging from such traditional parts of the liberal arts curriculum as French, German, history, and literature, to such highly vocational courses as dental assistantship, psychology for nurses, and foremanship. Many courses are in the curriculum in response to the demands of the supporting business and industrial community and are taken by nonmatriculated students. There are approximately 1200 matriculated students and between 800 and 900 students enrolled for one or more courses but not working toward a degree. Most of the students live at home. The degrees granted reflect something of the college's service and vocational orientation. In addition to the bachelor of arts, it offers the bachelor of music, of science, of science in education, and of science in business administration.

Especially since the move to its metropolitan location, the college has made impressive gains in student enrollment, financial support, physical plant and size and professional level of its faculty. It has, however, experienced difficulty in maintaining a consistent orientation. By tradition and through interests of the faculty, the college is concerned with the broadly liberal education of its students. Because of its support and the expectations of its present community, it is anxious to meet a variety of other vocational and cultural needs. Accommodating these two major efforts within its financial and staff limitations has provided one of the most persistent and perplexing problems.

While Institution A is chiefly a community college, Institution B is for the most part residential. It is affiliated with the United Presbyterian Synod of its state and is over one hundred years old. Almost from its origin it has dedicated itself to preparing educated Christians (for a time men only, but from the turn of the nineteenth century, men and women), liberally educated persons entering the ministry, religious service fields, and education. Although its curriculum has been broadened somewhat to accommodate other vocational needs, it still concentrates on preparing teachers, ministers, and an educated laity.

Being in a somewhat wealthier state, it has never faced the financial stringencies of Institution A. Though it is not affluent—few liberal arts colleges are—its existence was never threatened by lack of funds. Thus it has been immune from pressure for more and more vocational courses to attract students. Its curriculum consists of general courses in science, language, mathematics, history, and similar subjects, and some purely vocational courses in education, business, and home economics. It does offer prescribed curriculums for secretarial work, pre-library science, and pre-medical and dental technology and practice. These specialized curriculums, however, are chiefly specific patterns of the basic liberal arts subjects.

The institution has approximately 900 students who come from lower-middle and middle-middle income homes. Their parents are in the service professions and many of the students expect to enter such work. A large number live on campus, deriving therefrom many of the sought-for values of the college. Emphasis is placed on student government, on clubs, organizations, and fraternities, and on religious activities, which assume a large role in campus life.

Institution C is a small (175 students) girls' school conducted by a female order of the Roman Catholic Church and is located in a large industrial and urban community. It is young compared with the other two schools. It came into existence in the 1930's to provide for the collegiate educational needs of members of the sponsoring order. Gradually it expanded to offer liberal education for young Catholic women of that part of the state. Most of the students formerly lived at home, but the completion of a dormitory was expected to increase the number of boarding students. Relatively few young members of the Catholic order are being educated at the college. The chief vocational program is teacher education, but a good half of the student body takes a broadly cultural curriculum not specifically aimed at any profession.

C's faculty appears to be superior in training to the faculties of Institutions A and B. Further, its size in relation to the small student body results in a low student-faculty ratio. Classes are quite small and the institution has emphasized the virtue of intimate counseling both by members of the faculty and by professionally trained counselors. This intimacy, plus the social pressures of the girls' home community, has resulted in a campus life almost devoid of disciplinary problems. The same factors, however, have also militated against a vigorously effective program of extracurricular activities.

Institution D is also a small college (200 students) supported by another Southern Protestant church and located in a small, isolated, almost rural community. Its principal operations are conducted in a large multipurpose building; two dormitories house the majority of the residential students. Through most of its history its financial situation has been precarious, the college having been several times saved from ruin only by unexpected developments. One was the establishment of a community hospital on the college grounds, with an accompanying demand for a four-year program of nurses' training that brought a gain in enrollment and added resident physicians to the staff.

The curriculum of Institution D demonstrates the liberal arts background, with heavy concentration on music, literature, science, and mathematics. It also, however, shows a vocational orientation in its teacher-education program, nursing, medical technology, pre-theology, and business offerings. The students come generally from lower-middle and upper-lower income families within the state and denomination, and intend entering the service fields of education, the ministry, religious education, and social service. The extracurriculum, especially the religiously related activities, assumes considerable importance in the lives of the students. Since the community does not afford extensive recreational facilities, the institution must meet these needs of its largely residential student body. This task has proved somewhat difficult, in view of the conservative attitude of the denomination's state board of control. For example, it was only with careful manipulation that dancing on the campus was finally authorized.

It would be possible to describe similarly any of the some seven hundred such colleges in the United States. The four described, however, will suggest something of the variety as well as some of the common characteristics found among liberal-arts colleges.

The private, liberal arts colleges are small. They range from less than 200 students to as many as 2000 students, but they typically enroll less than 1000. This small size is regarded as one of their distinctive characteristics, one of their sustaining virtues. Their catalogues stress that the limited enrollment makes for small classes and personalized instruction to a degree that few other colleges can approach.

While the pattern is changing, these schools are still intimately related to one or several denominations. Even when a school has severed its direct connection with a church or denomination, typically it continues to stress its Christian orientation.

Although some liberal arts colleges of the type considered here are state supported, most are privately controlled and privately supported. Student fees provide slightly over 50 per cent of the cost of operating these colleges, and endowment another 20 per cent. Gifts and grants account for over 20 per cent of the total income for the very small Institution C (200 to 600 students), but less than 10 per cent for the larger colleges.[1] In the past the controlling churches contributed heavily to the support of their colleges. During the 1930's and early 1940's this support became nominal. It was in this period that a number of liberal arts colleges reorganized independently of any denomination. During the decade of the 1950's, however, serious attempts were made by church-related colleges to re-establish close ties with their denominations, these again making a rather heavy contribution to the financial strength of the schools. In a few institutions the re-establishment of close ties with the parent denomination saved the college from certain extinction. Since 1950, the private college has begun tapping an additional source of support in its individual and collective requests to corporations for unrestricted grants. So far this source has been increasingly productive, though its stability for the long-term future can only be conjectured.

Perhaps the greatest single common bond between the various liberal arts colleges is the purposes they claim to be seeking. Statements of purpose generally emphasize Christian scholarship, liberalizing studies, high academic standards, and preparation for the professions.

---

[1] *A Study of Income and Expenditures in Sixty Colleges—Year 1953–54* (Federation of College and University Business Offices Associations, 1955), pp. 26–27.

As a rule, such schools seek to provide for the general education of their students. This education is designed to produce mature men and women who will live by a consistent set of values and make effective use of their leisure time, not only for themselves but for the society of which they are a part. This general or liberal education is coupled with some concern for the vocational training of students; but how far the college should go in this direction is one of the debated issues. Many spokesmen for the liberal arts college contend that the broad general education it seeks to provide is really the best preparation for any of a variety of vocations and for all professional training. Both this liberal education and vocational training are frequently provided within a framework of Christian theology and philosophy. Those institutions still directly related to a particular denomination naturally make this framework explicit, but even those which have become almost secular continue to stress the Christian life.

The liberal arts college thus described is an exclusively American phenomenon. In England and in Europe, the right to confer the bachelors degree is restricted to institutions authorized to confer higher and professional degrees. In America, however, as a result of frontier conditions, of an essentially Protestant ethic emphasizing the need for an educated ministry and laity, of the necessity for early self-government, and of the prevailing philosophic climate of the seventeenth and eighteenth centuries during the nation's founding years, the liberal arts college emerged. Its primary task was to prepare an educated population which would enter the professions of law, medicine, and theology. As the idea grew that in a political democracy everyone should be educated, the relevance of the four-year liberal or general education became apparent. If a liberal education was good for the professions, why was it not also good for the rest of the educable population? (Clearly, however, this would still remain but a small proportion of the total population.) The rapid growth in the number of such institutions during the first half of the nineteenth century reflects this belief. By 1860, there were 500 colleges in the country. Although only 180 of the original institutions still survive, it is significant that in the following decades the total number of colleges rose by only 250. Actually, the liberal arts college was a development of the eighteenth and nineteenth centuries. Its characteristic form was established in those years. The many similar institutions created in the late nineteenth and early twentieth centuries have used the earlier ones as their models, frequently with no modification to fit the changing times.

Liberal arts colleges, molded to meet the demands of one period of history, have been faced with a variety of problems as they continued into subsequent periods. Originally they provided some of the functions now performed by the public high school. Indeed some of the early colleges were scarcely distinguishable from academies or secondary schools. Their curriculums were designed to meet the needs of a relatively small number of educated men and women in a few professional fields. As American technology began to expand, as other influences on education—such as the research orientation—began to be felt, in short as American society began to change, the liberal arts colleges began to encounter serious obstacles to their further development.

Some of these obstacles or problems were commonly faced by all kinds of institutions of higher learning. Whether it was a liberal arts college, a normal school, a land-grant university, or a private university devoted to research from the turn of the twentieth century onward, the institution had problems of student population, of curriculum, of research, and of faculty to solve. Some of these problems have acquired new significance since World War II, but all have their roots in earlier decades of the century.

Perhaps the most dramatic problem is that of greatly expanded student enrollments. Higher education in America had been based on patterns presupposing a relatively restricted and homogeneous population from which its students would come. These students would have shared a common intellectual tradition which implied considerable contact with books and with ideas. The pattern also presupposed that the graduates would enter one of a limited number of vocations. As the ideal of universal education became ingrained in the American character, as the society demanded more, and more varied, technical services, and as the ethnic groups comprising America became more heterogeneous, higher education was faced with a challenge it has not yet fully met. How provide an integrated education for a mobile and constantly changing population? How expand to accommodate ever-increasing numbers of students without losing the valid attributes of earlier forms of education? How provide a common cultural heritage for students coming from variegated cultural backgrounds? These are serious questions for which answers are being sought.

Particularly since World War II has the problem of numbers become a pressing one. From the experience of a declining birth rate in the depression decade of the 1930's and from the fact that immigration had been curtailed to a trickle, it was generally supposed that the United States was approaching a static if not a declining population. The dramatic upsurge in the birth rate and reduction in the death rate after World War II, however, placed the United States population among the fastest growing ones in the world. These expanding families, imbued with the American ideal of the values of college education, have begun to exert on all colleges a pressure from which no relief appears in sight. American society has apparently decided that its youths should have as much education as they are capable of assimilating. (Some would say even more than many can assimilate.) It has decided that at least half of all of its young people should receive some form of collegiate education. It has looked to the colleges and universities to meet this need, poorly though those institutions were prepared to do so. Further, while vigorously exerting pressure for colleges and universities to provide education, American society has not yet thought through the means for supporting this desired service. The problem, then, faced by all institutions of higher learning is to supply adequate instruction for many more students than ever before without a proportionate increase in subsidy.

But the financial problem is only one among many demanding solution. A second problem is a definition of the role of higher education in contemporary society. What is it that American society expects its colleges to do? Does it want them to produce skilled technicians for the various vocations created by an industrial society? Does it want them to provide students chiefly with a general education, leaving to some other agency the task of technological training? Does it want colleges to inculcate particular values or does it want them to leave such matters to the home, the church, or other social institutions?

Today higher education is in greater turmoil than at any other period in its history. For decades colleges and universities have been expanding their curriculums in response to a mutiplicity of demands for vocational preparation. From training lawyers and ministers, colleges moved to training teachers, home economists, engineers, journalists, salesmen, accountants, nurses, and policemen. Recently the validity of such specialized education as a function of a college or university has been challenged. Should not the colleges, it has been argued, give students a general education, leaving to professional schools or to the business and industrial community the task of training in specific skills?

Allied with this has been the question of whether the college should be concerned exclusively with the student's intellect or consider also his physical and spiritual development. Here again experience has varied. During the early nineteenth century college teachers devoted much time to the out-of-class life of their students. Each teacher conceived of himself as a guardian of his student's moral as well as intellectual attainments. Gradually this conception fell into disuse as college teachers tended to plunge back into their own research as soon as they had dismissed their classes. There is evidence that a reversal is in progress, though the extent of the responsibility colleges should assume in guiding the whole life of students is still debated. The decision will depend to a degree on the size of college enrollments.

Still another problem confronting higher education is that of finding and maintaining adequate staffs. It is one of the accidents of history that the population from which must come the teachers to teach the students born after World War II represented the smallest birth rate in this country's history. There are fewer people from whom to recruit college teachers at a time when colleges need more teachers while, simultaneously, American society requires more doctors, lawyers, architects, and other professional personnel to meet a demand for increased services. The seriousness of this problem is revealed by the fact that the 1953–54 percentage of 40.5 college teachers holding the Ph.D. degree was expected to drop to 20 before 1970.[2] How to provide the services society expects of them, in the face of this decrease in trained manpower, plagues public as well as private institutions throughout the country.

Stemming from the numerical problem of staffing is that of the role the faculty member should play. By the end of the nineteenth

---

[2] *Teacher Supply and Demand in Universities, Colleges and Junior Colleges, 1959–60 and 1960–61* (Washington, D.C.: Research Division, National Educational Association, 1961), p. 13.

century the stereotype, at least, existed of the college professor as essentially a research person. The Ph.D. degree was regarded as the passport into the profession, an entry gained through rigorous training in research methods. Further, in the larger institutions and to some extent in the smaller ones, continuing research and publication were regarded as the means toward professional advancement. If current trends in enrollment persist, however, greater and greater faculty energies will be demanded to meet undergraduate classes. As professors are required to meet students and instruct them in elementary subjects, the stereotype of the research professor will be brought into question. Certainly there will be losses in faculty morale as professors foresee a different role from the one for which so many of them trained. Whether or not high morale can be regained and faculty energies redirected has yet to be seen.

If college professors are to be expected to teach more students and do so effectively, some scrutiny of the methods to be employed is predictable. Again, the tradition from the nineteenth century has been that any productive scholar was by the fact alone presumed to be an effective teacher. And perhaps there was some justification for this belief, since many if not most college students entered the learned professions, and working under a research-minded professor was not unlike serving an apprenticeship. But the heterogeneity of present and anticipated student bodies ensures that students will leave for almost any of the hundred-and-one vocations now being practiced in America. Professors will no longer be master researchers teaching students their technical skills, and will thus be forced to rely on methods of teaching never before considered important. The very fact that the practice of teaching will be studied with a view to its improvement holds critical significance for all colleges and universities. As one example, it seems clear that television will have a major impact on the practice of education. Fitting this new technique into traditional college teaching methods will bring serious dislocations.

The small, privately supported liberal arts college is faced with all these problems. In addition it is faced with some problems peculiar to the kind of institution it is. At one time such colleges educated all students in the nation seeking collegiate instruction. With the rise of the large municipal, state, and private universities, each year has seen a decrease in the percentage of college students enrolling in the small four-year institutions. In a sense these institutions have become a minority group in the presence of a majority composed of other, larger and more complex types of institutions of higher learning. This minority status carries with it certain unique problems, met differently by different liberal arts colleges.

From one viewpoint the privately supported, Christian liberal arts college is in conflict with some major values held by contemporary American society. These schools came into existence in an earlier day and were patterned upon the values of that earlier society. Our society has since changed, and its values have changed. To the degree that liberal arts colleges have not altered their original value orientation, they are at odds with their present environment. This is not to admit that such conflict is bad. One could argue quite cogently that adherence to earlier values by a small group of institutions may provide the way for a return of all society to those values. An analogy may be found with the role of some monasteries in Europe from the sixth to the twelfth centuries in preserving the spirit of inquiry which, when rekindled, led the way to the Renaissance. There is no question, however, that conflict exists.

First there is conflict between the Christian religion these colleges profess and the secularism and materialism of the total American society. While there is some evidence of a reawakening of religious feeling in the United States, there is even more overwhelming evidence that our society is in the midst of what Sorokin calls a sensate culture.[3] People are interested in the here and now. They surround themselves with material goods and use the possession of such things as the chief criterion for judging the worth of a person. Our prevailing philosophies are hedonistic and pragmatic. Even our art reflects a concern for things of this world as contrasted with the other-worldly concerns of other ages. Emphasis is placed on getting along with people as a way of making the earthly life more attractive. Standards of personal conduct are regarded as relative, varying from culture to culture and from age to age. Personal success in life, in marriage, in the vocations, together with security of job and income, are the goals sought by most Americans.

With respect to all these, the Christian tradition, especially as interpreted in the principal Protestant doctrines, stands in direct

---

[3] P. A. Sorokin, *The Crisis of Our Age* (New York: E. P. Dutton & Co., Inc., 1956).

contradiction. The Christian code views the earthly city only as a prelude to the heavenly city; material things are of scant importance as compared with spiritual things. It judges the worth of an individual in terms of his kinship to God; activities designed to achieve only pleasure are held unworthy because personal pleasure is of no significance when compared with the glory of God. The individual's own salvation should be his chief concern even though this brings him into mortal conflict with nonbelievers. Standards of personal conduct are to be strictly governed by doctrines laid down in Holy Writ or in learned commentary on that Writ. Personal success is of significance only if it reflects and is used to further the Kingdom of God. There can be no security until one has reached the security of heaven in union with God.

Colleges which attempt to live by such a Christian creed run into conflict at every turn. Both faculty and students have accumulated many attributes of the majority culture, yet are called upon to practice and to preach other doctrines. The tensions in the lives of these people cannot help but influence their approach to the institutionalized function of their college. Several examples may suggest the intensity of this struggle of opposed goals. Grades are sought by students, and promotions by faculty, even though their creed says these are incidental items. The Christian tradition is authoritarian, yet the teaching of secular science asks each person to question all things. Service to humanity is judged good by Christian standards, yet men and women are required by the culture to ask what's in it for them. Church-related schools find it difficult to reconcile these conflicting value systems.

A second conflict of values involves the liberal tradition of the colleges and the vocational orientation of much of American life. In the ideology of the liberal arts, students should gain a broad understanding of the major areas of knowledge and a sympathy for and an affinity with the intellectual life. Education is seen as the chief means of making men more humane. By acquaintance, then, with the worlds of the arts, sciences, languages and philosophy, men are expected to be more effective individuals regardless of the calling they elect to enter. The often quoted injunction is that they should know the truth and the truth shall make them free. Great emphasis is placed on liberating the mind of man through the curriculum. The life of contemplation and serious discussion is judged best for human beings.

Such a conception has its roots in the Greek way and in the Renaissance ideal of the educated gentleman. But neither the social conditions that nurtured an educated élite nor the leisure to practice the contemplative life any longer obtain. Most Americans, even the wealthy, expect to work at some paid vocation during most of their lives. They seek in higher education those knowledges or skills which will help them become proficient in the world of work. While recently there has been some evidence that college students accept as valid the goals and purposes of general education, there is still impressive reason to suppose that most students enter college as a way to vocational success. Indeed, the proliferation of departments and courses, especially in the applied fields of business, engineering, and education, suggests the pressures of vocationalism. Students frequently complain about curricular requirements which hold up their progress toward vocational preparation. Their parents make very real personal sacrifices so that the children may attain higher positions than they themselves did. The conflict, then, is between a concept of education as a liberalizing influence and a concept of education as vocational training. The liberal arts colleges feel this struggle much more acutely than the state universities, whose original charters leaned heavily toward vocationalism. The liberal arts colleges have not received such a mandate, hence must work out their own solutions to the problem.

A third value standing as an issue is the problem of centralization. Liberal arts colleges as they developed became small autonomous institutions responsible for their own evolution. Steeped in the individualistic tradition of frontier conditions, each felt free to go its own way. Again, this value of independence can be traced to beliefs prevailing when the pattern for such institutions was established. There was great suspicion of any kind of centralized control, and a feeling that westward relocation would be appropriate if such control were exerted.

By contrast, there has been in the supporting society a pronounced trend toward centralizing many of the significant aspects of life. Government has moved from the laissez-faire condition of the nineteenth century to its present crucial importance in the lives of all citizens. Small businesses and small farms are giving way to large corporations and large farms worked by modern technology. Large state and municipal universities have grown and continue to grow as the chief means of collegiate education. Indeed, the tendency noted since World War II of state universities to expand through branches in various parts of the state appears to be accelerating as they try to cope with larger numbers of students. These branches are controlled centrally. Even some of the liberal arts colleges have followed a similar trend toward centralization, as exemplified in plans for a Lutheran University that would synthesize much of the work of the smaller Lutheran schools.

A genuine conflict exists here. The liberal arts colleges are conducted on the belief that small size and independent operation are essential to achieve their purposes. Yet much of current American ideology suggests that all purposes can be better achieved through large, centrally controlled organizations.

Not only do the liberal arts colleges face uniquely these conflicts in values, they also encounter difficulties from their size and peculiar physical situations. Many, particularly those in the Midwest, were established before the main axes of communication and transportation became crystallized, and many found themselves relatively isolated as these axes went elsewhere. Carthage College in Illinois, Olivet College in Michigan, Cornell College in Iowa are examples. They find themselves difficult to get to not only by prospective students but by the flow of new culture as well. Many cultural attractions can be obtained by institutions situated on the main arteries of commercial travel at relatively slight cost. Such attractions are unattainable to schools off main arteries, except at considerable expense. Yet tradition, coupled with the heavy investment in physical plants, makes it difficult if not impossible for such schools to remove to less remote places.

Then size itself is critical. As human knowledge has proliferated, colleges have felt constrained to give curricular attention to its newer branches. Where there are large, heterogeneous student groups, the institution can do this without markedly increasing the cost of education. The small enrollments of the private liberal arts colleges will not, however, support continual expansion of offerings. Yet these schools feel the pressure for such expansion. They feel that to attract more students they need to offer more courses, which in turn raises the cost of education and must be met by soliciting more students or larger gifts.

This pressure for increasing size conflicts with the belief that small enrollments make possible the most significant achievements of the liberal arts colleges. Their leaders feel that the personal interaction between students and faculty, possible when groups are small, is one of the most vital ways of inculcating love of learning and respect for humane values. How to adjust the values of small size with the equally stringent needs for growth is a perplexing issue.

The small-size faculty made necessary by the size of institution, coupled with the need for variety within the curriculum, gives rise to a further difficulty. Typically, many departments in the small school consist of one person. Without the informed stimulation of colleagues working in the same discipline, such isolated educators are likely to become victims of intellectual stagnation. Nor can such men gain greatly from interaction with teachers in other fields, because the tradition of specialization and the need to keep abreast of recent scholarship force them farther and farther from a lay level of comprehension of their fields. Faculty members just out of graduate schools frequently testify that one of the worst features of assignment in a small college is the sense of intellectual isolation they experience.

Deriving from these problems of values and of size is the whole matter of competition with other institutions for students and for financial support. With the depression decade of the 1930's and the war years of the 1940's as part of their experience, the liberal arts colleges feel the need to enroll students who might otherwise be candidates at a teachers college or a state or municipal university. After all, with over half of their total operating budget coming from student fees, these smaller institutions must attract students or go under. In seeking students, many have felt constrained to compete on the terms established by the more rapidly growing institutions. Vocational preparation, widespread distribution of scholarships, emphasis on competitive athletics, use of bands and glee clubs to call attention to the college, and publication of elaborate brochures and booklets have all been undertaken chiefly to meet the challenge of other kinds of education. Some liberal arts colleges have organized departments of home economics in the hope of attracting five or ten students who might go elsewhere were such a program not available. Competition is similarly felt in soliciting financial support. The small schools must devote considerable efforts to asking from private sources support that state schools get by legislative appropriation. Most recently the large industrial companies have been seen as such a source, and intense pressure has been put on them for funds. Unfortunately, this search has not infrequently resulted in modifying programs to coincide with the needs of prospective donor corporations. Some schools, for example, have initiated scientific and technical curriculums that they could ill afford, in order to make themselves worthy of corporation giving.

In the discussion thus far, an attempt has been made to show the privately supported liberal arts college as occupying a minority-group status with respect both to the total society and to the sub-society of higher education. This should not imply that all such schools fit this category; but considerably more do than do not. Sensing that they are somewhat out of step with the prevailing social values, individual colleges have reacted in different ways to the problems of faculty, curriculum, extra-curriculum, finances, and administration. Succeeding chapters will examine some of these problems.

CHAPTER II

The Faculty: Problem or Potential

It has been frequently said that an institution of higher learning is only as strong as its faculty. Buildings may be old or new, simple or ornate, the college may be hard pressed or in a relatively comfortable financial condition, without altering the institution's character. But if the faculty changes from a strong one to one lacking in scholarship, intellectual stimulation, or teaching ability, the college becomes completely different. To understand the unique qualities of the liberal arts college and to appraise its strengths and weaknesses, some analysis of faculty problems must be undertaken.

The average professor in the privately supported liberal arts college is in his middle forties. He has had graduate work beyond the masters degree. In a fair number of cases he holds the doctorate, but as a rule he does not. His academic rank is at the associate professor level, with about half the total group in the instructor-assistant professor ranks and the other half in the upper ranks. He may or may not be teaching in fields in which he received his advanced training. He is married (the pronoun "he" is used advisedly because the large majority are male). He has come from lower-middle class homes, although a number derive from upper class groups and a few come from lower class homes. He has entered the academic profession for a variety of reasons. For some it is clearly a means of upward social mobility; for others, a way of life which they find comfortable. Some, having found it impossible to enter some still more prestigeful occupation, have entered the profession by accident. Teachers of counseling and personal psychology, for example, not infrequently are persons whose desire to enter psychiatry has been redirected into other roles. For many the sheer love of dealing with ideas or of working with young minds seems to be the significant motivation. For others, however, the opportunity to perform before a relatively captive audience meets some fundamental psychological need. Typically these professors decided late in, or after, their undergraduate schooling to enter college teaching.

In many respects the professoriate in the small liberal arts college reflects the characteristics of the society of which it is a part. While they embrace some values not shared by the total college-trained population, they appear to be more like than different from it. They are interested in material success and are frequently a little resentful at the greater rewards accruing to members of other groups. They are not as active in political affairs as many would suspect. Nor are they likely to be radicals in social or personal philosophy. At the time of a national election the professoriate will divide generally the way the national population divides in selecting a national president. The professor is somewhat more tolerant of new ideas than the total national population and is somewhat less antagonistic toward minority groups than his peers outside the academic pale. He is not, however, inclined to champion lost causes nor to do very much that will deviate from the culturally-approved patterns of behavior. In large majority he finds academic freedom to differ from the rest of society virtually unnecessary because he really doesn't want to differ. His church attendance and membership coincide with the wishes of the constituent public supporting his institution. While he does live longer than the population at large, he suffers from the same bodily and mental afflictions that beset others not within the ivy-covered walls. He may be slightly more susceptible to nervous disorders than other professional groups, although there is no good way of validating this judgment.

Within the professoriate itself, however, there exist major differences between individuals. With respect to a philosophy of education, the entire range of viewpoints can be found on the campus of almost any liberal arts college. Some teachers will occupy a rationalistic position with its emphasis upon postulate (often divinely inspired) and deduction from those accepted premises. Others, very probably the majority, combine rationalism with a concern for the values of the Western tradition and a faith in some empiricism so long as empirical data do not too seriously jeopardize traditional ways of acting. Possibly the smallest number of professors will occupy a pragmatic position, relying chiefly on induction from constantly changing data to provide them with generalizations concerning life.

With respect to their view of their profession, a similar range exists. A number of relatively successful teachers view their subject as of primary importance, with students simply as an audience on which to try out new ideas. To these men, research and the scholarly life are much more important than their teaching function except in their guidance of future research workers. Another segment views teaching students as the chief reason for existence. They are inclined to subordinate the importance of specific subject matter to the needs of students. They are more concerned with the techniques of teaching and with intra-group relationships than with techniques of scholarly inquiry. Still a third group sees the academic life from a somewhat hedonistic viewpoint. Both scholarship and teaching are important, but so is the pleasantness of social contact with other professors and of the cultural resources open to a college community. In general, members of each of these groups have effected a satisfactory personal adjustment to the teaching profession. A fourth group, however, has not done so. Almost every institution will have a cluster of persons who are dissatisfied with their lot: the scholarship of students is deficient, the prevailing cultural climate philistine, the salary schedule too low, or the administration too oppressive; students are a nuisance and so are the administrative requirements of grades, checking attendance, and the like.

A similar range exists with respect to altruism. A number of professors see their vocation as a calling not unlike that of a minister or priest. They accept such things as low salaries, long working hours, and poor office equipment as minor inconveniences to rendering service to their fellow men. In some institutions having very low salary scales there will be well-qualified persons who could double their salaries elsewhere or in some other field of work. They elect, however, to remain, feeling a sense of obligation to their institution and to their students. At the other end are a number of professors who feel virtually no altruistic motivation toward their work. Teaching represents a way of obtaining the best possible income with the expenditure of the least amount of energy. They see the role of professor as no different from any other laboring job, and feel quite justified in using all manner of bargaining techniques to improve their own position. They keep their credentials up to date and use national meetings of organizations of which they are members as sources for contacts for job opportunities. Probably the majority of the faculty members occupy a middle position. They realize some satisfactions from their service to their institutions and students. They are, however, alert to the economic needs of themselves and their families. They join organizations, such as the Association of American University Professors, which emphasize both the service aspects of the professors and the safeguarding of economic needs of its members. They are dedicated to the search for truth but not to the point where the search would disrupt their personal lives. They value their students as persons but feel no great compulsion to sacrifice personal good for them.

Typically the professor in an American college is in many respects a marginal man. He lives in a community but is seldom a part of it. While some teachers do take part in political life and community service, the large majority do not. They tend to find their social life within the limits of the academic community and not infrequently are critical of the different cultural standards of their noncollege neighbors. This feeling of isolation is, of course, intensified by the suspicion with which the nonacademic community regards them. They deal with abstractions and talk in language incomprehensible to the rest of their community. While most will buy their homes, they still give the impression of living out of a suitcase. Such a matter as burial, for example, tells something of how college teachers regard themselves. Quite frequently the remains of dead professors or their wives are returned to their place of origin. This, one can speculate, contrasts with the practice of doctors and lawyers to be buried in the communities in which they have lived their lives.

This marginality is further intensified by serious conflicts between reality and expectation experienced by many teachers. Most college teachers are trained in the large graduate universities. The models upon which they hope to pattern their behavior are their graduate professors. Their first jobs, however, whether in a liberal arts college or in a university, force them to teach elementary courses with little if any contact with the specialized field in which their graduate training was done. The restiveness thus occasioned results in considerable personal dissatisfaction and not infrequently in pressures upon the college to institute courses that will allow the teacher to practice his specialized skills. Probably an important reason for the proliferation of courses in the liberal arts college far out of proportion to student demand has come about through such faculty demand.

While the faculties of liberal arts colleges face many problems in common with their colleagues in universities, some problems are peculiar to the private college or are found there in an intensified form. Possibly most important are problems related to teaching and to the curriculum. As the liberal arts college has faced the challenge of new social conditions and the competition of the large universities and multipurpose institutions, it has expanded its curriculum. In part this expansion has been made to attract students, but it has also stemmed from the desire of professors to teach a greater number of specialized offerings. Whatever the cause, the result is that teachers offer a startling number of different courses each year. It is not unusual for a professor to offer ten to twelve different courses in a two-year period. The amount of preparation such an undertaking demands, if adequately done, is enormous. Since professors are limited as all men are by time and physical endurance, these different offerings become simply textbook courses. The organization is that of the textbook writer, and conducting the class reduces itself either to a lecture or to discussion over the textbook.

To the demands of many different courses are added those of heavy loads of classroom time. For the private liberal arts college, the average credit-hour load will be between fifteen and eighteen hours per week. This compares with the ten to twelve hours found in the universities. While the number of courses taught within this load may be relatively small, the student load per teacher will range from 75 to 150 different students in class each week. If teachers were to attempt very much individual contact with these students or to expect as little as one written paper each week, there would scarcely be time left for the teachers' own preparation or even a semblance of home life. Obviously such asceticism is not frequently practiced. Instead, personal conferences with students are limited to those few who seek out the teacher. Written work tends to be limited to midterm and term-end examinations, with possibly term papers required in advanced courses. Since time is so restricted for even the most essential acts of teaching, it is no wonder that attention to such things as evaluation or personal counseling of students is difficult to demand.

Deriving in part from the pressures of time are several other related problems. The professors in the liberal arts colleges don't use the libraries which their institutions provide. Librarians are constantly on the alert to find ways to stimulate greater use of these resources, yet circulation figures remain low for both faculty and students. Now this generalization obviously does not apply to all faculty members, nor even to all institutions. There are professors who spend one or several hours each day in library work and there are institutions whose library circulation figures are double the averages for that type of college. Further, there is some justification for the often advanced explanation that many teachers purchase the books and periodicals they need and keep them in their offices. In view of the financial plight of many teachers in the liberal arts college, however, it is doubtful that this is a widespread practice. Similarly, the amount of research by the liberal arts professor does not compare with that of the faculties of universities. The demands of teaching and committee work during the academic year and the equally stringent need to find employment during the summer precludes much scholarly activity. This would not be too disturbing were it not for the probable close correlation between scholarly interest of faculty members with their effectiveness in interesting students in academic matters. It is understandable that adolescent students do not develop deep and abiding interests in intellectual matters if their teachers can't find the time to engage in such work themselves. The lack of research activity, however, has another unfortunate consequence. Professors are trained for the most part in institutions which emphasize the ideal of research even above that of teaching. Thus a stereotype of the college teacher as a research person has emerged. Those persons who find themselves teaching in the smaller institutions are apt to experience a marked discrepancy between the view of themselves conditioned by their graduate training and the way they actually function in their professional situation. As they emerge from graduate school, the ideal of the researcher seems attainable. As the years pass by and the demands of meeting classes and selecting textbooks claim their energies, the ideal becomes dimmer, but leaves in its stead a sense of disillusionment. One can speculate that some of the criticism which these teachers level at secondary education, or even at the intellectual powers of their own students, results from projection as a defense against this sense of unfulfillment.

Related to such projection is another matter. For many liberal arts colleges, particularly in the Middle Western parts of the country, the preparation of teachers is bread-and-butter business. Indeed, in many such institutions, over half of the student body will be anticipating teaching as a vocation. Yet the preparation of teachers is seen as a reason for apology, and every professional demand of teacher trainees is grudgingly granted. Professors of education are suspected of being somehow less respectable than teachers of other subjects. State departments of public instruction are seen as enemies who want the traditional liberal arts curriculum to be emasculated in the interest of increased education requirements. College administrators trained in the field of education are criticized by their faculty members, who feel that their prestige as liberal arts teachers is diminished if they are asked to consider teaching methods or evaluation as of equal importance to the content of courses. Consultants brought to the campus to assist in curriculum revision have a much greater chance of acceptance if their own training happens to be in one of the older liberal arts fields than if they should hold a doctorate in education. The author, for example, was trained in history. Faculty members have told him that his remarks were received with greater attention just because of the field in which he studied. He may have said exactly what a professionally trained student of education might say, yet he was considered respectable while the educationist was not.

A second cluster of faculty problems faced by the liberal arts college is the matter of training. Regardless of the intrinsic validity of the Ph.D. degree, it has become accepted as the appropriate training for a college teacher. The privately supported liberal arts college has difficulty obtaining an equal share with the larger universities of teachers holding the doctorate. At the present writing the proportion of all college teachers holding the doctorate is slightly less than 40 per cent. The proportion of teachers in the private liberal arts college is under 25 per cent. This situation is brought about by several factors. First, the university is able to offer greater inducements to recipients of the doctors degree. The matters of salary, of opportunities to teach advanced courses, of the chance to do specialized research, all exert a strong appeal to the young man or woman just out of graduate school. For one beginning college teaching without the doctorate, the university also offers subsequent opportunities to earn a degree. If he accepts appointment in a university he can work out his doctorate, without the expense of moving, by carrying some course work in addition to his instructional duties. Except in those rare instances when a liberal arts college is located in the same vicinity as a university, such opportunities for further education do not exist for the teacher employed by a smaller institution. To further his education he must go away during the summer. Since his salary is scarcely adequate even for living on his home campus, seeking a doctorate under such conditions poses a hardship many potential degree candidates are unwilling or unable to accept. The result is that the liberal arts college has a less adequately trained faculty than the larger institution. In recent years, the problem has been magnified because of the competitive bidding by large state-supported institutions even for teachers well established on the faculties of the smaller colleges.

An earned doctorate is not the only way to competency in college teaching, of course. Many varieties of in-service training may be attempted. For example, in several universities newly appointed junior faculty members attend at least for a semester classes taught by more experienced colleagues. At others half a teacher's assigned load during his first year is comprised of visits to the classrooms of senior faculty members and to seminars on college teaching. The margin of personnel is so small, however, in the smaller institution that such solutions are just impossible. A new faculty member, regardless of his age, training, or lack of experience, is expected to carry his full share of teaching responsibilities. Since this is a fifteen or more hour burden, not much time is available for understudying older colleagues.

Another aspect of the training problem is the necessity for professors to teach in fields distantly allied with or unrelated to those for which they have specifically been trained. As the liberal arts college has added courses and programs to its curriculum in order to be of greater service to its constituency, it has not been able to employ adequately-trained specialists for all of them. This has meant that instructors not too well prepared have had to present such offerings. A teacher of history, for example, at one institution was asked to take over economics as well. The physics teacher in another college habitually is assigned the more advanced courses in mathematics. In still another school a woman professor of education was asked to head a newly created department of home economics. A variety of demands within fields is even more prevalent. Teachers of American history also teach Russian history. Speech teachers handle rhetoric, English teachers offer work in journalism, and the medieval scholar provides instruction on the modern drama.

Similar in scope is the tendency of some of the smaller institutions to rely on part-time instructors. A course in journalism is taught at the four o'clock hour by an English teacher from the local high school. The wife of the dean might teach studio art out of her own experience as a practicing artist. A local physician might offer the required course on hygiene. Wives of faculty members find themselves teaching part-time in some of the multisectioned courses of freshman composition or the social studies. Sometimes a husband and wife combination can be found in which each is fully qualified in some field of the curriculum. Employing both at modest salaries provides them with a family income which is competitive with that offered by larger institutions for either one. Typically, however, the part-time appointee is less experienced, less well trained, and less qualified than regular appointees. The use of such aides on the faculty appears to be a way of offering more courses at slight cost. The education thus provided is apt to be inferior, when judged by the prevailing standards of college education in America.

Although intimately involved in other categories of faculty problems, certain aspects of the financial situation of liberal arts college faculty members are worthy of separate comment. The most obvious generalization is that these teachers are not as well paid as professors in universities, multipurpose institutions, or state-supported teacher-training institutions. While there are regional variations, and while it is true that a few of the highest paid professors teach in private colleges, the fact remains that, financially, appointment in a private institution is less attractive than in a state-supported one. This fact makes for other problems.

The relatively limited salary budget makes it difficult for the liberal arts college to offer a significant range of salaries for the various academic ranks. In order to secure a share of the younger products of graduate schools, salaries are offered them which are close to the highest the institution can pay anyone. It is not at all unusual for a college to offer $5000 to $5200 to a new instructor holding the Ph.D. but having no teaching experience, while paying the highest salaried full professor $7000. Between the instructor, assistant professor, and associate professor level scarcely more than $200 a year might separate the respective salaries available. Such a situation offers slight encouragement for young, well-qualified teachers to devote their professional careers to that institution. They put in several years gaining experience and then search for more rewarding appointments. Many of the faculty members who are content to remain and accept the modest increments as they come along are the weaker ones, who contribute little to the progress of the institution. Some schools have attempted to solve the problem by relatively rapid advance in rank for young faculty persons. Such a policy, however, places a capable young faculty member at the full professor rank and at the highest salary bracket by the time he is thirty-five to forty. He then has several choices, all of them unfortunate for the liberal arts college. He may simply stay on, regarding his position as a sinecure. He may seek more attractive teaching posts—though, since he has not had time to do research to gain a national reputation, he must accept considerably lower rank at a larger institution in order to gain a higher salary. One can find a significant number of assistant professors in state-supported institutions who had been full professors at a private college previously. A third option is to move from the teaching ranks into administration by becoming a dean or a president. A fourth is to seek further advance outside the institution while retaining appointment within the liberal arts college. Doing translations for corporations, teaching in evening school, non-scholarly but well-paying writing or consulting jobs are some of the devices teachers have used to augment their income and increase their professional influence. Whichever option is elected, the liberal arts college stands to lose all or a part of the services of qualified faculty.

The scholarly life of teachers is one which requires relative tranquility. They cannot be expected to devote their best energies to their professional work if they are worried about paying for even simple necessities. As one visits a number of liberal arts colleges, one is struck by the proportion of teachers who are in serious financial situations in trying to exist on their salaries alone. Professor X is an example. He taught languages in a college of 600 students. He was forty years old, had a wife and three children. His rank was full professor and he was paid a salary of $5000 a year.

He had achieved his Ph.D. after marriage and had had a number of school debts to repay. He rented an older house, possessed a five-year-old car, and had savings consisting of $300 worth of U.S. savings bonds. He wanted to do research in the summertime, but found that in order to provide for his family he needed to work. Since the demand for language teachers is not great, he typically accepted manual labor or routine clerical work each summer. Since his college could offer him no brighter financial future, he eventually had to move.

Another example is a thirty-year-old professor of philosophy. He had taken a degree in theology, found himself uncomfortable in the ministry, and had returned to the university for a graduate teaching degree. Family needs forced him to discontinue after two years. An able person, he was appointed to a strong liberal arts college at $4000 a year salary, but since he did not possess a doctorate he could not expect to advance in rank there, and his salary did not allow the luxury of further graduate work. Thus he is faced with the choice of remaining where he is with a future of low salary, moving to a weaker institution for the sake of a few hundred dollars' increase in salary, or leaving the teaching profession. With such choices open to him, his teaching is likely to be less than fully creative.

There was a time when liberal arts college faculty members could accept such financial straits and still evolve rather secure lives for themselves. College professors came then either from rural areas or from the upper-middle or lower-upper classes of urban society. In either circumstance the possibility of inheriting from one's family were great enough to provide eventually the requisite financial security. As the social demands for higher education have increased, however, college professors have been recruited from social classes unable to provide such inheritances. The stipends paid do not allow younger faculty members from lower class origins to establish a firm financial footing. Without this, an insecurity is engendered which must have its impact on the quality of their teaching.

Although the benefits of the Teachers Insurance and Annuity Association, created by the Carnegie Corporation, have gradually been extended to many liberal arts faculty members (and an increasing number are now eligible for Social Security benefits on retirement), the financial condition of retired professors is still not particularly secure.

The general financial insecurity of the liberal arts college faculty member has definite effects on his professional life. Not only is he forced to seek non-professional employment in the summer, or to do a great many chores such as painting his own house, but he is frequently prevented from keeping abreast of his own field. In America one keeps pace with developments in scholarship through reading, particularly in the learned periodicals, and through contact with colleagues at national meetings and through correspondence. Many of the smaller institutions do not have adequate resources to purchase needed journals for the library. From a library budget of $3,000 to $4,000 a year for acquisition not much surplus is available after encyclopedias, essential monographs, and the more popular periodicals and services are purchased. Travel money is used in taking the president on his various public-relations and fund-raising ventures, and very little remains for faculty members to go on trips to the large metropolitan areas where national and regional meetings are usually held. Help with correspondence is similarly difficult to obtain. A typical pattern involves secretarial help for chief administrative officers and a small secretarial pool for the teaching faculty. It is difficult for a faculty member to conduct any sort of consistent correspondence with workers in similar activities elsewhere, and even more so to maintain files which would make such correspondence meaningful.

If the institution cannot support these necessary activities, they must be paid for by the faculty member himself if they are to exist. An average salary of $6,000 for a middle-aged teacher with a wife, three children, and a belief in the future education of his sons and daughters, does not allow for many trips or many subscriptions to journals. A full teaching schedule does not yield the time necessary to write one's official letters oneself. If one's wife does not type or resents doing clerical work free of charge, one just lets interesting correspondence projects go.

For institutions intended to be centers of intellectual activity, many liberal arts colleges are far from being ideal. When colleges were established in the eighteenth and nineteenth centuries, little attention was paid to transportation facilities. A college would be located in some town or hamlet in the expectation that young people from the immediate vicinity would come by foot, wagon, or horseback with plans of staying in residence for the full term. Roads and turnpikes, railroads, highways, and airline terminals, as they developed, of course reached towns and cities in which some colleges were located. They missed more than they hit, however, because many founders of colleges, to keep the young collegiates from the temptations of urban life, selected sites likely to be off the paths of commerce and transportation. At present the colleges which lie some distance from principal transportation routes are in a virtual intellectual *cul de sac*. A college in Illinois is thirty minutes by car from the nearest trunk rail line and an hour from the closest airport. Another school in Iowa is twenty-five minutes from the nearest rail and air facilities. A half dozen colleges in Arkansas are accessible only by car or bus, as are many of the schools in West Virginia. The difficulty of access to these places results in several problems. Many students will just not attend colleges so hard to reach. Professional lecturers, concerts, and other cultural events are difficult to schedule because of the travel time involved. Some schools, though relatively isolated, have more fortunate circumstances. One institution lying on the main east-west rail line about one day's travel time from Chicago obtains a rather sophisticated cultural program quite inexpensively because the town is a natural stopping place for groups heading for the West Coast. Another institution, seriously restricted from commercial transportation facilities, uses private planes and cars to bring speakers and entertainers to the campus. These, however, are exceptional conditions not open to a large number of colleges in small towns. And the locations of these colleges deter sister institutions from sending representatives to conferences and similar activities which the colleges might attempt to sponsor. Just the lack of hotel space makes it almost impossible for one college in an Ohio town of 500 to convene professional groups for longer than half-day meetings. If it is difficult for colleagues to visit such institutions, it is similarly difficult for professors at them to go elsewhere for meetings.

But even more serious in contributing to an intellectual isolation in smaller institutions is the composition of the faculty. As these colleges have tried to compete with the universities with respect to curricular offerings, many departments have been created, each manned by one or possibly two persons. Thus the exchange of ideas among men working in the same field, which makes university departments such vital organizations, is not possible in a smaller institution. Yet the tradition of separate disciplines and departments has become so thoroughly entrenched in American education that even one-person departments are perpetuated. If whoever occupies this position attempts to keep in contact with the world-wide developments in his field, he loses ability to communicate with his local colleagues in other fields for all save the commonplaces of local living and campus politics. If he tries to make common cause with his local peers, he may fall behind in his own discipline.

Teachers in large metropolitan areas or in universities possessing substantial financial resources have available a variety of intellectual activities. Museums, libraries, industrial research centers, theatres, galleries, and the better examples of these on tour can help the professor keep an open mind. Obviously institutions in smaller places or financially feeble cannot give their faculty or students advantages. Not having them with any regularity means that the habit of using them becomes weak. Thus even when, at considerable expense, important orchestras or speakers are brought to an isolated campus, the local response is likely to be meager. When the faculty and student body fail to patronize cultural events, the college administration feels reluctant to make future sacrifices of funds so sorely needed for plant maintenance or other pressing purposes.

A final problem of faculties in the smaller liberal arts college is the discrepancy between their training and what they are expected to do. Most probably, they obtained their graduate training in universities, where the ideal of research is deliberately inculcated, and teaching is typically regarded as less rewarding than research. The young graduate, as he leaves for his first position, has been thoroughly indoctrinated. If he accepts appointment in the smaller institution, he finds no time for research and little encouragement to do it. He is assigned heavy teaching duties, frequently of introductory courses. He is expected to supervise student extracurricular activities and in many schools to conform to the local mores of church membership and community service. All of these are worthwhile activities, but they differ widely from the young professor's expectations. He may respond by forsaking research, and feel no qualms about it. Or he may become bitter. One of the most pitiful plights is the man who never has been able to adjust his role, as faculty member on a liberal arts college campus, to the expectations he formed while a graduate student. He wants to move, yet has fallen so far behind that he cannot qualify for the places he would like to go.

It should be clearly stated that while these problems are quite generally encountered, there are notable exceptions both on individual campuses and in entire institutions. Many men lead full, productive lives as teachers and scholars and suffer few ill effects from working in a small institution. Some of the most stimulating colleges in the country are small institutions, isolated geographically. What has been described, however, are the problems likely to be experienced unless deliberate steps are taken to prevent their arising or to solve them. That they can be solved is the author's faith and belief.

With respect to the financial condition of faculty members, a variety of measures have been taken by some colleges, and could be taken by others. While considerable attention has been given to fringe benefits for faculty members, the first concern should be to raise faculty salaries.

The liberal arts college generally receives its support from student fees, from gifts and from endowments. Some lifting of the salary level can be made by increase in student fees. Unless the resultant hardship on students or their parents is alleviated, however, an increase in tuition can force students to the lower-cost state-supported institution. Offering students non-interest bearing notes, payable within a stipulated period after graduation, for a part of increased fees is one method. Allowing parents to start paying tuition costs several years before a student enrolls, or letting them pay the tuition on a monthly instead of a lump-sum basis, is another possible technique. Another method would be to use all tuition money to pay for the instructional program, and make this fact explicit in the literature the college distributes. If this were done, support for administrative overhead and for the building and plant maintenance program would have to come from endowment and by making such activities as the dormitories self-supporting and self-liquidating.

All schools whether or not they can risk major adjustments in tuition can do other things to obtain money for higher salaries. Within almost every institution there are many courses and programs which do not contribute to its essential purposes. There are also programs with a disproportionately high cost as compared with its other offerings. It is relatively easy to assemble cost data for each course and each program. This information together with figures showing the yearly enrollments in each course, plus some sensitivity to the purposes of the institution, can provide a rational basis for re-examination of the curriculum. For example, it might be found that several courses in the social sciences attract few students each year. If these courses were eliminated, it might be possible to provide as vigorous a program with one-half or less of a faculty member's time. Or it might be found that the music department requires 8 per cent of the annual instructional budget while providing service for only 2 per cent of the student body. Elimination or modification of the music offerings could free the salaries of several faculty members, which could be applied to the more basic aspects of the curriculum. Again, special teachers may have been hired to offer a major for which no real student need existed or which the institution was unable to support adequately. An example might be a small college (with 300 students and 30 teachers) beginning a major sequence in home economics. If the college has embarked on many such ventures, the resources which should be used for the school's essential purpose become dissipated. Major surgery on such parts of the curriculum can provide financial savings to be devoted to improving salaries.

Other managerial techniques than curriculum revision are also appropriate. Much instruction which is carried on in multiple small sections can be handled in larger units. Once the initial cost of closed-circuit television has been met, student cost for multiple section courses can be reduced as much as 50 per cent. Combination of small departments into larger functional divisions can result in savings on overhead which may then be applied to salary funds. Curtailing student dropouts or attrition is another possibility. Typically, about 50 per cent of the students who attend liberal arts colleges drop out of school before graduation. The largest proportion of these leave school within the first two years. With each student who leaves school the institution loses its overhead investment in him—money and time spent for recruitment, admission, and organization of courses at the freshman and sophomore level. If this attrition rate could be reduced, some appreciable savings could be made despite the fact that upper level courses cost more to offer than lower level ones. Such means as improved advising, a stronger instructional program, and better criteria for admission are all helpful.

Increasing salaries is only one solution to the economic plight of college teachers. Other economic benefits would materially help—making available to them home-building lots at nominal sums, helping finance their homes, providing rental apartments, and letting them purchase goods through the college. Assistance in the educational expenses of children of faculty members or for the further education of the faculty member himself would also be welcome. A few institutions have subsidized graduate training of young people holding the bachelor's degree, with the understanding that they will return to teach for a stipulated time. Retirement plans, health insurance, and life insurance are other benefits which can insure the financial well-being of college teachers. More difficult is to provide for faculty members who become incapacitated for extended periods through catastrophic illness or who are required through reasons of health to curtail their activities.

Requirement of a complete physical examination as part of the procedure for initial employment, and encouragement of the use of the college-financed student medical center for annual physical examinations for all faculty may help prevent some situations from becoming serious. But those which do should be anticipated by depositing each year out of general operating budgets, an amount that can be drawn against for salary payments to seriously ill faculty.

But to solve the problems of the liberal arts college faculty, more is needed than simply improving their financial condition. Ways must be found to help them grow as professional persons. Here a number of techniques have been tried, some with considerable success. Having faculty members return to the campus a week before school opens and then providing leadership for them to think through their educational plans is one way. Maintaining an adequate professional library and giving administrative encouragement to study or reading is another. Every college should develop and maintain a faculty handbook to be put in the hands of every teacher. The content of such manuals will vary, but they all ought to list duties and responsibilities of teachers, describe procedures such as purchase of supplies, and clearly state the philosophy of the institution. In addition, some periodical bulletin containing a calendar of coming events on campus, routine administrative announcements, and social announcements should be distributed to every faculty member. Various specialized documents should also be prepared.

Sometimes faculty members can best be led to improve themselves if their institution participates in regional or national cooperative enterprises. Out of the North Central Association Study on Liberal Arts Education, for example, have come important changes in faculty thinking. Schools which participated in the American Council on Education Cooperative Study in General Education or the Cooperative Study of Evaluation in General Education, reported considerable faculty growth. Of course, many of the things faculty members did in those projects could be done alone; but the prestige of being part of the Study, and the feeling of responsibility for commitments made in the name of one's institution, seemed powerful incentives for faculty members. Even such relatively small matters as sending faculty members to inter-college meetings, or asking them to report to the total faculty, afford recognition which in turn motivates faculty growth.

Another consideration in the further development of the faculty's professional competence is the publication of their scholarly output. If teachers feel there is a good chance their research will be published, they have a powerful motivation to do the requisite work. Providing such means can take the form of an institutionally subsidized journal of scholarship and opinion. It can take the form of small grants-in-aid for faculty to do research. It can consist of providing clerical aid for scholarly work, or of under-writing the purchase of a given number of copies of books if a professor's manuscript is published. If the institution allows salaried time for the preparation of textbooks for students, royalties can be used to subsidize publication of scholarly work of more limited appeal. Several institutions have initiated mimeographed bulletins publishing scholarly work of its faculty, and a few have modified the medium of the alumni news to publish faculty writing. One institution has fostered a monthly research meeting at which professors read papers in the fields of their special interests.

Perhaps nothing is so crucial to the long-term success of the institution as the improvement of college teaching. The research tradition in American higher education has been so marked that it is only recently that the teaching facet of the professor's role has even reached parity with his research function. By now, however, a number of techniques have been tried and proven reasonably successful. They range from using student evaluations of teaching, class visitation, and research and study on college teaching, to reducing the class load so that adequate teaching can take place.

To reduce the amount of intellectual isolation of faculty in smaller liberal arts colleges requires great effort by trustees, administrators, and the faculty itself. Several guidelines, however, can be tested. First is a reorganization of the faculty into larger administrative units. There is something pathetic about a one-man department of chemistry or of history. The professor in such a unit spends much of his energies just trying to keep up with a program that attempts to compare with university departments. It is doubtful if a liberal arts college of 500 students can offer departmental majors in more than four or five fields. If, however, the fifty-man faculty were divided into six or seven divisions, divisional offerings could be quite rich and profit from the thoughtful discussion of the six to ten men comprising each unit. If the division is given realistic administrative and curricular power, and if attempts to proliferate back into departmental compartments are resisted, this larger unit can make for a genuinely creative experience for its members.

If colleges are supposed to be intellectual centers in American society, they must deliberately plan to assume such a role. If an institution is located off the main transportation routes and at some distance from the metropolitan areas, it has that much greater obligation to augment local resources with imported talent. A lecture, concert, or cultural events series is but one device. Providing museum exhibits, recording and replaying significant programs from the mass media, or developing opportunities for local talent to perform are all possible. Whatever means are used, the faculty should be encouraged to take advantage of what is offered and to work it into the texture of the courses they teach.

Inviting experts from off campus, employing distinguished visiting professors from time to time, and sending faculty members to visit interesting programs are also means of improving the intellectual tone of a faculty. Perhaps some of the travel budget allotted to the administration could with good purpose be diverted to faculty travel to conferences or other centers of education. Only as channels for the free flow of ideas between faculties of different institutions are opened can provincialism in liberal arts colleges really be reduced.

CHAPTER III

The Curriculum: Visions and Distortions

The liberal arts college curriculum, as it developed in colonial and early American times, appears from this distance to have had a real unity and integrity. It was an institution brought into being to communicate, to a relatively small proportion of the population, the major strands of the cultural heritage they would need in assuming the positions of leadership in society. Courses in the classics and in moral and natural philosophy were judged the essential components of an indivdual's education whether he entered the ministry, the law or, to a lesser extent, medicine. Classical learning and languages formed the heart and provided a common body of allusion with which educated men could communicate under all circumstances. Probably this liberal arts curriculum as it was actually practiced demonstrated many malfunctionings. The curriculum occasionally could be arid, the teaching of early college professors —or, as frequently, college presidents—would more often than not degenerate into simply moral or ethical exhortation. The very balance of the curriculum, poised on the fulcrum of classical learning, carried within it the seeds of ultimate curricular rigidity. In spite of such weaknesses, however, the curriculum and the college itself proved effective and turned out generations of highly literate individuals who could put together the monumental political documents of the eighteenth century and could create an indigenous intellectual tradition in the nineteenth century.

In the twentieth century, however, this historic unity and integrity have become distorted and diffused in its effect. And this distortion is reflected in a number of developments characterizing the curriculum of the liberal arts college. The first of these is the amazing multiplicity of courses and the specialization of the arts and sciences far beyond the needs of undergraduates. It is presently commonplace to find departments in liberal arts colleges offering two and three and four times as many credit hours of work as are required for majors in the subject. In history in addition to the broad courses of American, English, European, ancient and medieval, small liberal arts colleges will offer specific courses on the Civil War and Reconstruction, history of the West, history of American participation in World War I, history of science, a local history, and many others. The English department has offered courses obviously on Shakespeare, on the pre- and post-Elizabethan dramatists, courses on Browning, on the 19th century English novel, and on the recent American novel. Physics moves from general college physics through mathematics and thermodynamics, electricity and optics, radio and electronics, atomic and nuclear physics, civil aeronautics, and meteorology. Chemistry will frequently be represented by organic, qualitative organic, and physical chemistry, and languages will run the gamut from those elementary skills courses to such specialties as 19th century Spanish literature.

This proliferation of courses nowhere reaches such heights as in the departments of music in the liberal arts college which have become essentially conservatories of music rather than programs meeting the liberal arts needs of its students. One institution, normally restrained in its course offerings, nonetheless offers counterpoint, history of music, orchestration, conducting, and form analysis to top off an already full program of music prerequisites.

One gets the impression, in looking through catalogues of liberal arts colleges, that they are in a definitely competitive relationship with the large graduate training institutions. One of the more respected liberal arts colleges which prides itself on its conservatism offers to students Anglo-Saxon literature, the earlier Renaissance, Tudor drama, Jacobean drama, Milton, Restoration literature, the age of Pope, from Jonson through Blake, Wordsworth and his contemporaries, Byron, Shelley and Keats, as well as the broader courses on period literature.

The reasons for this proliferation are not hard to determine. There is the tradition of the research institution which has infiltrated the liberal arts college. Its teachers, trained in the large, complex universities, have brought with them their notions of what is appropriate college-level work. They were able to inject these ideas into the curriculum of the small college by holding up the specter of the condition of students when they reached graduate or medical school without such specialized experiences. The fact that the graduate schools really don't care has rarely been investigated. This whole development, deriving from the early part of the present century, gives the impression that the initiative for what properly belongs in the liberal arts college shifted to the supposed needs of a handful of students who might ultimately find their way into advanced study.

Even those liberal arts colleges which try to make their curriculum more appropriate to the needs of general students have not been successful. In recent years, a number of these colleges tried to follow the lead of some of the state universities in creating programs of general education. By and large they have embraced the form of this more broadly conceived undergraduate education, but missed the substance. In effect, what has happened is that the liberal arts college has superimposed a group of broadly constructed courses on top of its normally specialized curriculum, staffed these with the youngest, least experienced teachers, and then given the students the option of taking the general courses or the specialized ones. Thus, students were allowed the odd choice of a broad course in social science or a course in research methods in sociology, either of which was supposed to contribute to the student's general education. The imperative criterion for an effective program of general education, that it actually replace many of the courses in the liberal arts curriculum, rarely has been realized in the kind of institution being discussed here. The resultant tension caused by student overload is normally resolved by assigning less and less significance to the general education courses.

Again, there are reasons to explain this situation. General education courses frequently have been mixtures of barely related bits and pieces from older subjects. They as frequently have been poorly taught and not unusually have been simply watered-down versions of an older introduction to a specialized sequence listed under a new title.

This distortion also is revealed in the misleading, if not actually fraudulent, statements about the curriculum made in many liberal arts catalogues. Some courses creep into the curriculum because of the interests of a professor. When he moves on, retires, or dies, the course title remains although there may not be anyone who can really teach it. The subterfuge of a statement at the front of the catalogue that a number of the listed courses will be offered on demand is scant justification for perpetuating this practice. An even more vicious aspect of this problem is the tendency of a number of schools actually to offer a highly specialized course with a professor who is not qualified to teach it. Again, the way of course establishment is similar. A new professor, having completed his Ph.D. in a specialized aspect of English literature, is given the privilege of teaching a course on his thesis, partly as a fringe benefit the institution offers. And this is not necessarily a bad device. Faculty morale is important, and allowing a faculty member to profess openly a subject to which he devoted two years of his life is sound practice. However, when this specialist leaves the institution, it is almost fraudulent to ask another individual having only slightly more than a layman's knowledge of the specialty to teach the subject.

Another reflection of this deviation of the liberal arts curriculum from its purpose is found in the lack of any formal or informal integration of the curriculum. The liberal arts college in the eighteenth and nineteenth centuries made its impact on students because it was essentially a unity and students could see, and were shown, the relationship between moral and natural philosophy, between the languages of the ancients and their philosophic beliefs. This integration has virtually disappeared and professors don't seem to care whether or not courses in history, language, anthropology, and science add up to a single penetrating experience in the lives of students. In 1957, the writer tried to identify liberal arts colleges which had really become concerned about the problem of the integration of educational experience. Eventually he found a few somewhat atypical institutions that recognized this problem. However, even the efforts of these few seemed artificial in view of the amazing variety of courses which capstone courses, senior seminars, comprehensive examinations, senior theses, and the like were supposed to bring together.

Another aspect of distortion, certainly related to all that has been said, is the fact that the curriculum has exceeded the personnel resources of many liberal arts colleges. A typical pattern in such a school is for faculty members to teach fifteen to eighteen hours a semester. This load will normally involve several sections of some broad undergraduate course and several specialized courses. The next year the pattern is the same but the specialized courses change. In effect, professors in liberal arts colleges will normally claim to teach, in any two-year period, perhaps eight or ten or more separate courses. Few scholars can keep abreast of the research in this many different subjects even though they all be somewhat related. As pointed out earlier, the resultant teaching device of simply covering the textbook is almost an assured outcome of such an approach to curriculum building. Further, the sort of curriculum being discussed here is terribly expensive. An institution that offers two or three times the number of courses needed by students majoring in the subject is forced to quite small classes, each costly to maintain. Ruml and Morrison have pointed out that at least part of the financial plight of college professors is due to their insistence upon teaching so many different subjects.

A last item of distortion involves the relationship of the liberal arts college curriculum to the increases in knowledge. This relationship frequently takes one of two distinct forms. Either newer branches of knowledge are not included, on the grounds of lack of respectability, or newer groupings of subjects are heaped on top of an already full offering. Some of the courses in social psychology, microbiology, the newer mathematics, are too often rejected on the pretext that students really need the traditional courses. They are as frequently rejected because faculty members are unwilling to reorient their classes to accommodate these newer matters. Or if the institution moves in the other direction, if it has faculty members who can up-grade their own education, the new learning is added to all the old learning. The demand of science departments for more and more of students' time is a direct result. Nuclear physics is placed on top of the old materials of Newtonian physics. Theory and history of numbers is placed on top of trigonometry. Courses on communism and the modern world are added to courses on history of the ancient world. With such a process of constant addition and rare subtraction, the liberal arts college is bound to develop a curriculum which has no integrity, no meaning for large segments of the student population, and very little real substance.

The drift of the liberal arts curriculum away from a focus and into its present overburdened and amorphous state has come about as a result of a number of forces and pressures. First, as the land-grant and state colleges began truly to flower and to offer a variety of specialized vocational courses, the liberal arts college has felt itself constrained to compete. Although the private liberal arts college rarely operated primarily on tuition, tuition did make up normally about 60 per cent of the operating budget. Student fees were thus not unimportant. The very reason for the existence of a liberal arts college was to educate students, and as the state-supported institutions expanded, the liberal arts college offered more and more courses so that they could make the same claims as the more comprehensive institutions. It is impossible ever to know, but one can speculate that the programs in home economics for a college of 500, the business administration courses, and certainly the teacher preparation courses, were by and large created to attract those students who might otherwise have attended a normal school or one of the larger state-supported institutions.

This vocationalism is exemplified not only in such offerings as nursing, business, or education, but in the more orthodox liberal arts offerings as well. Each of the liberal arts departments would argue that students should major in their sequences in order to prepare for some vaguely related vocation. Thus social workers should take the sequence in sociology. Prelaw students obviously should have a political science or history background. Premedical students, in addition to basic chemistry and physics, ought to have considerable zoology and physiology. Salesmen certainly needed speech, and workers in the various governmental bureaus needed majors in whatever specialty they thought they wanted to practice. The fact that having a particular major was really irrelevant in large numbers of vocations into which products of the liberal arts colleges went, the fact that law, medicine, and dentistry not infrequently had to undo the education received in a related undergraduate subject was rarely considered. It was enough to argue *a priori* that students who were going to work in a penal institution should have twenty-five or thirty semester hours of sociology, or that a surgeon should have had comparative anatomy as an undergraduate. Combine this point of view regarding the values of the liberal arts curriculum with an expanding number of vocations existing in the society and it is inevitable that the curriculum should become out of balance.

A second force has been the real or sensed demands of accrediting agencies and certifying bodies. While the over-all impact of the great regional accrediting associations such as the North Central, the Middle States, or the Southern Association have been positive, their very existence has contributed, and continues to do so, to certain strictures in the curriculum. If an institution decides to offer a major in some subject, the accrediting teams obviously try to compare the course offerings with those of the very best in the region. If the University of Illinois had courses in experimental psychology, an accreditation team member might raise a quizzical eyebrow if an aspiring liberal arts psychology department did not also have a roomful of rats, and mazes in which they could perform. Even when the accrediting agencies are doing their best to foster a broad kind of undergraduate education, when they are asserting their prestige and influence to allow each institution to develop in ways consistent with its own history, this point of view still operates. For example, when one of the strong institutions for women in the Middle West was given a routine review visit, the members of the team kept harping on the fact that the major areas of concentration for students did not resemble completely those in elaborately organized universities.

Even more hurtful to the liberal arts curriculum have been the real or supposed demands of the professional accrediting and certifying organizations. One wonders how many unnecessary courses in chemistry have become lodged in the liberal arts curriculum simply because a professor assured a curriculum committee that the American Chemical Society demanded such and such a course. One can also wonder about the proliferation of courses in accounting, if the graduates of liberal arts college X were to be allowed to sit for CPA examinations. This expansion of the curriculum through fear is perhaps nowhere more clearly exemplified than in the professional education courses. Normally state departments of education require between eighteen and twenty semester hours of technical courses in pedagogy. Yet it is commonly accepted doctrine that the excessive demands of state certification make mandatory an additional year of schooling or serve as justification for the inclusion of extremely specialized courses in education. This is an insidious process.

A new institution was created several years ago and attracted to its administration a number of individuals well known because of their criticisms of the distortions having crept into collegiate education. They decided that this new institution would not be caught in the trap into which had fallen so many less informed administrators. The state was not excessive in its certification requirements, demanding only twenty-one semester hours. The first four-year catalogue of this institution listed, in addition to the obviously necessary courses of educational psychology, methods courses and practice teaching, such specialties as psychology of exceptional children, education of retarded children, of gifted children, techniques of educational research, school curriculum development, tests and measurements, and theories of learning. The rationale for the inclusion of each of these courses was the demand of the state certifying agency, although such was not really so.

Allied with the two previous factors is the belief on the part of many professors that their curriculums must provide full coverage for majors. No person, in their estimation, should go forth with a major in history unless he had sampled the major divisions of history, had had specialized work in most of them, and had taken courses in method and historiography as well. No student should be surrendered to medical school until he had thoroughly mastered a major sequence in chemistry with course titles similar to the subjects a Ph.D. candidate would be studying. The fact that a liberal arts college can really do nothing more than kindle an interest which can be exploited by the individual throughout a lifetime of further study rarely enters these discussions. Nor is consideration given the fact that a number of these highly specialized courses either teach materials which become obsolescent before they could possibly be used, or contain such irrelevant specificity that students forget what they have covered almost as quickly as they leave the final examination room.

The liberal arts curriculum is an extraordinarily effective demonstration of cultural lag. Practitioners of academic subjects struggle for years, or generations, to make their subjects respectable enough for inclusion in the curriculum. Once having achieved success, these subjects continue even though the reasons for their existence have long disappeared. Classical languages are included in the curriculum of many liberal arts colleges because they have been there, and because they are respectable. Whether or not a truly competent teacher of Latin and Greek is available and whether or not the classical languages have real significance in contemporary society is not questioned. The sciences came late to a favored position, but now the major subjects of chemistry, physics, and mathematics, and the minor ones of geology, astronomy, and the biological sciences are firmly entrenched. The fact that some of these, with propriety, could be replaced by some of the newer multinamed subjects is occasion for great debate. Clinical psychology has finally become established. But social psychology, communication theory, or human behavior are still suspect and are admitted to the curriculum only with reluctance. The aphorism that changing a liberal arts curriculum is not unlike moving a graveyard is true enough to illustrate this cultural lag.

It appears that the job of the liberal arts curriculum is not sufficiently afflicted by the troubles thus far discussed. In addition, some of the newer educational ventures are made to seem most attractive. During the 1940's a number of the big universities, which educated large numbers of engineers, agriculturalists, business majors, and the like, sensed a need for a common liberal arts curriculum for all their graduates. The significant programs of general education at the University of Minnesota, Michigan State University, the University of Chicago, and Harvard University came into existence. The argument in favor of general education seemed so persuasive that a number of the smaller liberal arts colleges became convinced they, too, should have such programs. Institution after institution adopted general education courses, not in replacement for something in the curriculum, but as an offering on top of everything else. The result was almost ridiculous. Students were required to take as much as 50 per cent of their work in prescribed courses, yet the curriculum continued to proliferate and offer more and more specialized courses each year. Instead of saving resources, which, properly organized, general education can do, its advent in the liberal arts curriculum resulted in still more expensive undergraduate education.

Similarly, the liberal arts curriculum has been augmented by some of the educational fads which come and go so rapidly. On top of an overflowing curriculum have been added honors seminars, senior colloquia, tutorials, and interdisciplinary faculty-student projects. These, together with remedial reading or other improvement courses, are not necessarily bad, but become so when they are added to an already chaotic pattern of variegated courses, resting on equally varied educational theory.

The inclusion of specialized courses in the liberal arts subjects results partly from an unfortunate correlation of the scholarly interests of faculty members with the substance of the curriculum. The example of the German research scholar has led the American professor astray. That stereotype shows the German professor doing research on the frontiers of knowledge and then sharing the results and his methods with apprentice scholars who are the university students. This conception may make sense in terms of European education. In the English sixth form, the French lycee and the German gymnasium, the general education of students is provided for. The university is, in some respects, similar to the American graduate school. Hence the mode of teaching should be appropriate to advanced specialized work. In the American system, the general education of educated people is assumed to be a joint responsibility between the secondary school and the undergraduate college. The general education of individuals demands that their needs be of primary concern in establishing the curriculum, rather than the need of a professor to share his research. Furthermore, in spite of the widely held belief that American professors are essentially research oriented, one can seriously doubt whether the majority of professors in liberal arts colleges actually do any research beyond that for their doctoral degree. What this amounts to, then, is that the American scholar builds a curriculum as though he were in a European university, while the needs of the students are for something else and his own competencies are inadequate for what he builds.

It could very well be argued that the scholarly activities of faculty members should have no one-to-one relationship to what they teach. There is really no reason for a professor to insist upon teaching a course on minor Restoration dramatists solely because he is currently writing a book on the subject. Michigan State University has, for many years, maintained a Basic College (called more recently University College). This has offered a required core of general education courses offered by professors who teach full time in that college. The faculty of the Basic College has consistently had the highest, or second highest, proportion of Ph.D.'s in the University. It has further ranked among the top several colleges in the production of scholarly works. This suggests a model which private liberal arts colleges might follow.

One of the strongest forces for increasing specialization of curriculums in the liberal arts college has been the departmental organization and the disciplinary loyalty of faculty members. Again, the basic stimulus may have been the German research professor. Translated to the American scene, the department as an adminis- trative unit has sought to justify larger staffs and more budget through offering increasing numbers of courses and searching out larger numbers of majors. If a student might become a major in a subject, but was deterred because of the absence of some one course, by all means add it to the curriculum. This empire-building tendency is reinforced by the feeling of loyalty of professors to their discipline and to their department rather than to the institution as a whole. American professors think of themselves as historians or chemists or psychologists, rather than as teachers or professors at institution X. They get their feelings of prestige and status from following the proceedings of, or attending when funds permit, national meetings of their disciplinary peers, and they get their opportunities to progress in the profession by developing a kind of service reputation. Unfortunately, they translate into curricular terms the frontiers of their subject that occupy the conversation of the leaders of their discipline.

One last pressure needs to be mentioned, possibly one of the most significant forces resulting in curricular distortion. This is the presumed requirements of the graduate schools. In curriculum committee after curriculum committee across the country, chemists, sociologists, psychologists, and political scientists argue vociferously for the inclusion of advanced, specialized courses in the under- graduate curriculum because their students will need these courses when they enter graduate school. The fact that only a small number of students from most liberal arts colleges enter graduate school, and the needs of the majority should determine what everyone re- ceives, is not considered. Further, the exact relevance of these advanced courses for subsequent training in graduate school has rarely been questioned. In this whole region there is a great deal of misunderstanding and misinformation. Knapp and Goodrich showed some years ago that a small number of privately supported liberal arts colleges prepared a large number of subsequent graduate stu- dents. Undoubtedly those liberal arts colleges turn out students who successfully do advanced work. The largest number of students in graduate schools, however, took their undergraduate training in large universities. The majority of graduates from most liberal arts colleges in the Middle West, the South, and the Far West enter elementary or high school teaching. The sorts of courses these students need are decidedly different from those presumed to be needed by future graduate students. Yet those presumed needs determine what the future public school teachers shall study. One must also examine whether even the presumption is valid. Bernard Berelson in *Graduate Education in the United States* cites a growing tendency for graduate schools to accept students regardless of their undergraduate major. There is even slight evidence that the graduate student is somewhat more successful if he has had a major quite unlike the work in which he will specialize during his advanced study.

These are all potent forces in the direction of distortion. Some palliatives, however, are feasible and are worth trying. There are some means by which these forces have been blocked and occasionally redirected. Perhaps the most important is an institutional self-study. Here the accrediting agencies are being a creative force by urging colleges to be reviewed periodically and to prepare a self-study in preparation for this review. A self-study, carefully conducted by an entire faculty and digging into all aspects of an institution, can reveal some of these malfunctions. In such a study a faculty normally asks itself, what are the institutional objectives and what are the objectives of the various divisions and departments? And are these mutually consistent? Then the self-study committee on curriculum can examine each of the course offerings to determine whether the course reasonably contributes to the achievement of this major objective. A self-study properly done gets into the matter of finance; and a curriculum committee may very well realize that the faculty's curricular myopia is costing them and their families dollars, for the inclusion of every single course costs money.

Vigorous administrative leadership is another way of bringing about curricular reform. In the American tradition, virtually all curricular reform has come about through the energies and insight of administrative officers. In another connection, it has been argued that in American institutions, progress results from the dynamics of the administrator encountering the conservatism of the faculty. This point is repeatedly borne out in the history of education. Elliott's free elective system, Wilson's renovation of the Princeton curriculum, Hutchins at Chicago, and Hanna at Michigan

State University are all examples. The administrator in the private liberal arts college can do a great deal to change the curriculum and make it more sensitive to both the history of the institution and contemporary needs. To do so the administrator must be willing to use all the powers of persuasion and of sanction which his position allows him. The administrator in the American college is legally the executive officer of the board of trustees. As such, he is responsible for the employment of personnel and the expenditure of funds to achieve the institutional objectives. Prudent exercise of the powers thus implied can result in miracles of reform.

A third remedy involves the full imposition of budgetary analysis and budgetary control to curricular problems. It is currently possible to determine rather precisely the cost of education in the various courses, departments and divisions within the institution. If the institutional budgetary officer can make continuous cost studies of the entire educational program, the faculty may obtain needed information to consider realistically whether a continuation of certain parts of the curriculum is worthwhile. One can imagine that a thorough cost analysis of a liberal arts curriculum might show that home economics and music are costing twenty to thirty times as much as the courses in history and sociology. Faculty curriculum committees can then ask themselves, is the perpetuation of such expensive offerings worthwhile? Occasionally they may be, but at least the decision is made in the full awareness of what a disproportionate cost for one part of the curriculum means to all other parts and to the institution as a whole.

The educational world at present is in flux. New journals, conferences, workshops, research reports, monographs, and discussions are generating as many new ideas about education as at any period in the history of the enterprise. Many of these notions will prove ineffective and will drop by the wayside. Others, however, will stand the test of time and become an essential part of American education. It is unfortunate that many liberal arts colleges are off the main arteries of transportation and communication, and that a number of them have insufficient resources to send their teachers where they can obtain new ideas. But more can be done than many might believe. For years the North Central Study on Liberal Arts Education provided workshops in the summer to which representatives of liberal arts colleges could come to have their visions of education lifted. The Danforth College Community Workshops have attracted other professors. Grants made by the major foundations, and opportunities for travel under Fulbright and other federal grants, all are means of helping faculty find out more about education. An institution, even a small one, might with propriety designate some funds each year as risk capital to let some of their faculty travel for new ideas about the curriculum.

Another remedy lies in asking faculties to give closer attention to the emerging needs of society and of students. In suggesting this, one does not argue for a constantly changing curriculum, but for a curriculum a little more sensitive to the real needs of people than has been true so far. If an institution does send a number of its students to graduate school, some quantitative study of what those students actually need would help solve many a curricular battle. If the institution exists for the sake of a specialized clientele, the needs of that clientele should be studied and known intimately. For instance, an institution which draws on essentially a noncollegiate trained population has different problems from those encountered by some of the East coast colleges whose students virtually all come from college-trained homes. Of recent years the literature of social criticism has grown, and there are appearing important insights about the conditions of society and how education could serve this society. As an example, the Presidential Commission on Purposes and Goals for American Society, the various projects of the Rockefeller brothers, could be studied with benefit by those responsible for the collegiate curriculum.

A last suggested way of mitigating some of the worst distortions is based on an analogy to human experience. If an individual deliberately sets out to do friendly things and to appear cheerful, he not infrequently alters his emotional tone in the process. A number of directive therapists suggest such disciplines as thinking happy thoughts or trying to do nice things for others as a means of moving a patient out of the depths of depression. At first these acts are highly artificial, but therapists testify that if the patient perseveres and is not too deeply disturbed, improvement will come. It may be that the liberal arts curriculum can be improved by the imposition of a few arbitrary devices for integration. Obviously, with as much wrong with it as is true of the liberal arts curriculum, the imposition of a senior capstone course is not going to make a great deal of difference. But if this course is imposed and maintained long enough, the idea of restoring integration may take hold. Similarly, a comprehensive examination may create more problems than it can possibly solve at first. Yet if a carefully prepared comprehensive examination is given to all students and continued for some time, its very existence may lead professors to think seriously about the inter-relationships among their various subjects. Artificial stimulus may lead to profound change.

While these suggestions can bring about improvement in the curriculum, they are at best remedies for symptoms, and no matter how carefully applied, will not affect the basic malaise of the liberal arts curriculum. To do this requires a new synthesis or a new theoretical structure for such programs. Possibly, the time in history is now ripe for such a formulation. It must rest on certain assumptions or postulates.

The first of these is that the undergraduate school, and especially the liberal arts college, is essentially a method of advanced general education. The case for this may be argued from several points of view. It is probably true that in the years ahead the time we spend at work will be drastically reduced. At present in all save some of the highly professionalized vocations such as medicine, the work week of the educated American seldom exceeds forty hours. We can expect this to be reduced to thirty-five, then thirty and twenty-five as the various automatic devices make themselves felt. The task of education is not to prepare people for work as such; it is rather to prepare them to use the vastly increased hours at their disposal for leisure. The kind of education that prepares educated men and women for work is likely to be the kind that can be best offered on the job or in the technical and professional graduate schools. If this assumption about the needs of society in the future is accepted, the consequences for curriculum reform are immediately apparent and are significant. The vocationalism, the specialism which has characterized the liberal arts curriculum in the twentieth century can be rectified.

A second postulate is that no one during the undergraduate years can presume to study all or even a majority of the aspects of a complicated subject. To attempt to do so is to tilt at windmills. Even the stable subjects based in history have become so large that a student in four years' time can do no more than sample a few representative blocks of the curriculum. Thus the curriculum planners for the liberal arts college should realistically remove from their minds the search toward complete coverage. Rather, they should approach their problems as Eric Rogers did years ago in analyzing the science program and developing the block and gap system. His science courses made no attempt to cover all the major scientific problems. Rather he selected a few which seemed to be relevant to the lives of students, susceptible of projection into major principles, and of easy transfer to other situations. Students studied these on the assumption that in later years if they saw a need for filling in the gaps, they could do so with the tools which concentration on the blocks developed in them.

A third postulate is that people with a collegiate education should properly understand the various approaches to knowledge but need not necessarily study numerous examples of each. One can conceive of knowing as extending from pure sense of perception to intuition, extrasensory, and revelational knowing. If students have experienced these to the point where they can accept their validity in certain situations, the college education has done its job properly.

A related postulate is that students need a variety of kinds of educational experiences but do not necessarily demand constant exposure to these experiences. It is well that a college student have a deep and intimate relationship with some faculty member with whom he can share not only intellectual concerns, but personal ones. This does not require that students should have a tutorial relationship with every one of their instructors. Similarly, it is well that students have some experience with the use of laboratory equipment. But how many test tubes must a student break before he realizes that test tubes are of glass? The college curriculum based on this idea could provide the whole range of experiences which students need. To attempt to duplicate experiences in each of a number of subjects is expensive and not necessarily productive of efficient learning. Perhaps this point should be made explicit with an example. Students working in the social sciences do need some experience in gathering information, but there does not appear to be enough difference between a research course in psychology from one in sociology or education to warrant separate course offerings.

Still another highly significant postulate is that students should be required to concentrate on but a relatively few courses at a time.

There is some evidence that even if required to take five courses in a semester, students normally concentrate on two or three, relying on native ability and shrewdness to get through the less interesting ones. If an institution were to set up a curriculum in which students took no more than three courses in any one semester, but probed these courses deeply enough to understand their full ramifications in actual life, the number of college courses in the curriculum would be reduced to a manageable figure. It would be possible to bring about true integration, and students might come closer to the English or Continental ideal of real mastery of a subject.

A sixth postulate is that the undergraduate college need not concern itself unduly with the prerequisites for graduate education. This means that each level of education has its own unique purposes, goals, or mission, and that the next higher level is responsible for relating its program to the kind of product the lower level produces. It means that the high school should not attempt to prescribe to the elementary school, which has its socially approved purpose of developing the basic intellectual skills for learning. The collegiate institution does not tell the secondary school what should be in its curriculum, for the secondary school has a major task of providing the rudiments of general education for a national population, the passing on of major cultural values, and the initial steps of inducting young people into adult living. Similarly, the graduate school cannot expect to, nor in fact does it, prescribe the functioning of the undergraduate institution. There is mounting evidence that students can enter graduate school or even the highly specialized schools of medicine, dentistry, and law from any of a variety of undergraduate majors. Students entering medicine after a bachelors degree in philosophy have to do a little concentrated work in their first year of medical school, but it doesn't seem to affect their over-all performance. If this bugaboo of the demands of graduate school could be exorcised, the chances for thorough revision of the undergraduate curriculum would be immeasurably enhanced.

One further item needs to be mentioned although possibly not with the dignity of a postulate. This is that as a general rule no department in a liberal arts college can afford to offer more than about one and a half times the number of courses actually required for a major. If a major is thirty hours, forty-five hours should be the most that the college catalogue would list. This allows ample latitude for student individual differences yet keeps the number of courses within manageable proportions.

With these postulates in mind, it is possible to visualize the liberal arts curriculum. Many writers have used the analogy of the wheel, and the temptation to do so again is too great to be by-passed. At the center of this wheel would be a core of courses similar in purpose, if not in nature, to those found in effective programs of general education. There might be one course in the natural sciences, one in the social sciences, one in the humanities, and one in the realm of communication or language arts. The precise number would vary with the kind of institution. A Roman Catholic college, because of its religious mission, might include five courses, the fifth one religion and dogmatic theology. This core of courses would be normally taken during the first two undergraduate years. Alongside these courses, and intended to provide students with an awareness of the broad dimensions of knowledge, there would be more highly specialized courses aimed at teaching the epistemology of the major divisions of knowledge. These specialized courses might parallel exactly the general education courses or exceed them in number, grouped into clusters related to each of the general offerings. The outside rim of this wheel would be the specific application courses.

Obviously, this analogy of a wheel has more relevance for some parts of the existing curriculum than for others. One can speculate that beyond the social science course would be a course in historiography or philosophy of history, and outside of that the several empirical courses such as United States history, history of Europe, of Russia, etc. Beyond the humanities course would be courses in aesthetics or literary criticism and outside these, the specific courses in English literature and the like. Outside the social science courses might be the theoretic courses in education, followed by the practical courses in pedagogy. Foreign language could conceivably be built with direct relationship to the language arts. As one analyzes the existing offerings of a liberal arts curriculum in terms of such a structure, one begins to discover clearly defined parts of the curriculum which should be eradicated for the good of the entire organism. Careful pruning in terms of a definite conceptual scheme may be the way for the restoration of balance, harmony, integrity, and purpose to the liberal arts curriculum.

CHAPTER IV

Student Personnel: Problems of Balance

The attitude of collegiate officers toward their responsibilities to the out-of-class life of students has fluctuated from extreme, almost parental concern during the eighteenth and early nineteenth centuries, through a laissez-faire attitude in the late nineteenth and early twentieth centuries, to a renewed preoccupation with such matters. In the early period the president and his few associates felt personally responsible for the religious life of students, their moral development, and their ability to support themselves in college. By the time of the renaissance of interest in student out-of-class life, most institutions had become too big and complex for faculty or administration to feel personally responsible. Management of even the smaller institutions demanded much of the president's time. Faculty, loaded with hours of contact in classes and with keeping up with new horizons of their subjects, had little time or inclination to assume further burdens. It was to provide for students' needs outside the classroom that the student personnel movement was born. To man the newly created positions a variety of student officers came into being.

In view of this history, it is small wonder that the large institutions were among the first to create student personnel services. It was in these institutions that the impersonal research emphasis reached its most complete expression. The faculties could daily see that their students were somehow missing important elements in their development into adulthood. They saw clearly that special officers would have to be appointed if the university were to provide adequate services of this sort. If the large, multipurpose institutions were to be something more than intellectual factories, it had to provide ways of selecting, admitting, and orienting students, and to care for their needs as human beings.

Once the student personnel movement was under way in the universities and its officers not only caring for the needs of students but training future officers as well, the idea spread to the smaller institutions. Frequently it did so through the assumed obligation of large institutions to supervise, or at least judge, the effectiveness of small colleges. If separate offices for student personnel activities were desirable for a state university, they were equally worthwhile for small colleges. This led to several developments.

The small liberal arts college has adopted many of the student personnel activities. Non-accredited institutions seeking recognition from their approved sister institutions have followed the suggestions of the manuals for accreditation and have created the necessary position or offered the suggested services. But generally they have not evolved or accepted any consistent theory of student personnel work, just as a good number of larger institutions have failed to give significant focus to such efforts. In this regard, the liberal arts college is in a much happier situation concerning its curriculum. Although the underlying theory of its curriculum may be outmoded or may never actually have been effective, nevertheless it embodies a philosophy that can be used as a criterion of what to include. To some it may be the concept of the medieval trivium and quadrivium. To others it may be the stereotype of the English curriculum at Oxford or Cambridge. To still others it may be the classical program of the early colonial colleges. No such prior conception exists for the student personnel efforts. This means that as new fads have come along, the smaller institution too frequently has added a social director, a coordinator of housing, an admissions counselor, or a dean of women without really giving thought to how the total undertaking should mesh with the rest of the institution.

Further, the small liberal arts college has generally been unable to finance full-time staffing of its student personnel activities. It has depended upon faculty widows for house mothers, teachers of psychology for counselors, and other individuals to take on student personnel work in addition to their regular duties. Such a procedure, while not ideal, could provide adequate staffing if a reasonable time adjustment were made. However, the already mentioned heavy teaching loads intrude. Thus a teacher may have his load reduced from eighteen to twelve or fifteen hours in order to serve as a registrar. Another person may be relieved of one course to head up a testing program. Since each of the functions usually requires specialized knowledge and the three or four separate courses still being taught by the individual also demand specialized preparation, the result is too often routine, pedestrian performance of all roles. These heavy pressures may even result in serious emotional strain for men and women of good will who, at least as students, saw excellent professional performance. It is indeed frustrating for a part-time dean of students to hear of the newer approaches attempted in more affluent institutions and know that the realities of time and energy will forever deny him the chance to try them.

Occasionally a smaller institution will decide that some aspect of student personnel work deserves a full-time officer. Here the present-day competition for the better trained workers becomes felt. Too frequently the institution must appoint an inadequately trained or inexperienced person to the post, or one whose personality or effectiveness is less than desirable. The havoc such an appointment can create in an institution just reaching awareness of need for more services is sometimes remarkable. One small institution in Pennsylvania appointed a full-time Ph.D. in psychology to be the director of counseling. He had drunk too deeply at the Freudian well and filled his statements to the faculty with the analytical jargon. "Deep therapy," "ego supportives," and "birth trauma" became nasty words on the campus. His effectiveness was so impaired that he had to leave at the end of one year, and it was five years before the college could try again. Obviously, the small college is not alone in making inappropriate appointments. But the high visibility of a student personnel worker in a small institution makes a poor choice there more damaging than in a bigger community.

Nonetheless, small liberal arts colleges have persisted in developing the attributes of a student personnel program. While the number and intensity of activities undertaken vary from college to college, as well as whether a particular activity is considered student personnel, there is reasonable uniformity in organization. There is also, unfortunately, uniformity in some of the weaknesses in the various features of the program.

Recruitment and admission of students are obviously necessary for all colleges. With some outstanding exceptions, private liberal arts colleges state that they admit students who graduated in the upper half of their classes and have good moral character. This ideal, however, is tempered by the real imperatives of filling dormitory space or even classroom space. In practice, students from any rank of their high school graduating class can gain admittance into any of a number of liberal arts colleges. Even those who have not graduated can also get in by demonstrating minimal performance on such tests as those of General Education Development. It should be indicated that the self-studies completed by many liberal arts colleges state that the institution hopes to become more selective in the future, but the evidence does not suggest that this is happening.

There are certainly many forces at work to create this easy access. The constituency of churches of a number of liberal arts colleges is small, and hence the number of young people interested in college is also small. Colleges do have facilities which must be used. They do have faculties which must be paid and a charter to which they must adhere. At least some of the problem, however, is intensified by linking the recruitment with the actual decision-making about admission. Thus the salesman has the power to decide which candidates should be accepted. Since his primary emphasis is placed on filling the dormitories, his judgment may be overly influenced by non-educational concerns. The reality of this criticism can be seen in the changing complexion of some of the smaller Midwestern liberal arts colleges. Increasingly, their student body is composed of large numbers from the Eastern seaboard states where the large private institutions are becoming genuinely selective and where state-supported institutions have lagged behind those in other parts of the nation. Those students, excluded in their own region, are being recruited to fill the places in Midwestern colleges of better native students .who elect the Midwestern tax-supported colleges and universities.

Once admitted, students are next exposed to orientation to college life and to the testing program. While a few colleges arrange orientation sessions in central places in the summer before students enter college, the normal procedure is to set aside a few days to a week just before the opening of school. These periods are filled with testing sessions, exhortations about how to study, dances, mixers, rushing by Greek letter societies, and registration. Rarely are the intellectual concerns of the college made explicit to students during this period. Testing consists of administration of academic aptitude tests, English placement tests, and the like. It is in regard to these that the tendency for such colleges to accept the form, but not the substance, is pronounced. Tests are given because every good college gives them, but the data are rarely used except for required reports and all too frequently not even for that. It is shocking to visit a number of institutions and find that no official can generalize as to the relative abilities of his own student body.

College historically has been viewed as a means of preparing youth first for the learned professions, and more recently for a wide range of other vocations. Thus the college is expected to help its new students decide on a career. Presumably, some of the testing done during the orientation week is intended to help students assess their abilities as they decide what vocation to enter. Unfortunately, many of the tests included have their primary value in predicting success in a curriculum rather than suggesting where an individual's ultimate interests and competencies might lie. It is a rare liberal arts college that does what one institution has done—post odds on student success in each of several vocational curricula at the time students begin to think about registration. In addition to the testing data, some office is charged with collecting vocational materials that may stimulate student interests or answer questions about the educational requirements they must meet. Where this file of materials is located is almost as varied as the number of liberal arts colleges in the country. There may be a vertical file of vocational leaflets in the library, in the office of the academic dean or dean of student affairs, in the alumni office, or elsewhere. Not many students know where they can go to find such information; one has the feeling that students may be guided even less with suitable information about vocations than they are in mate selection.

Perhaps one important weakness in the vocational guidance part of the student personnel program in the liberal arts college is the mistaken notion among so many faculty that the majority of students will go on to graduate school. An institution may send no more than two or three of its graduates on to advanced study, yet the curriculum and the motivations provided students assume that all will go. The matter of placement is not an unrelieved picture of ineptness. In few institutions, however, are the real vocational aspirations of the student body studied and appropriate materials and advice given.

Also under the general heading of vocational guidance is the placement of graduates. Since the small, privately supported liberal arts colleges—with the usual exception of those along the Eastern seaboard of the United States—serve primarily as teacher-training institutions, placement efforts for teachers have been developed at least to some extent. Frequently this work is handled in the department or division of education, with the person heading that unit also serving as the placement officer. The effectiveness of this effort is impaired by the limited time he can give to it. In one- or two-man education departments, the problem of staffing needed courses, supervising practice teaching, and keeping track of state certification requirements takes priority over the task of placing students upon graduation. Nevertheless, the institutions do manage to get their graduates placed. Much less thoroughly developed is the placement for other vocations. It is a rare institution that has set up a placement office to coordinate the recruiting efforts of prospective employers and can keep students informed of employment possibilities. A normal procedure is to spatter a bulletin board with typed, printed, or mimeographed notes of job opportunities or of an impending visit of a representative from some corporation.

Another major area of student personnel includes student housing and the fraternity system. By and large, the smaller liberal arts colleges have been established in small, somewhat isolated communities—partly, as previously mentioned, on the belief of founders that keeping students away from the temptations of urban centers was good. Thus the majority of colleges of this sort are residential institutions, which supposedly should have developed quite intensively a residence-hall system. This simply has not been so. In college after college in the Middle West, until the advent of the college housing program of the Federal government, residence halls were inadequate physically and in their staffing. One can at least theorize that the almost rank growth of national or local fraternities and sororities on small liberal arts campuses came about because the college had not met its obligation to provide residence halls. If the Federal college housing program continues, it is likely that the residence-hall needs of these liberal arts colleges can be met. However, staffing them with adequately trained personnel is a different matter. Here the institutions are caught with a problem which plagues all residential institutions.

There is the strong belief that a residence hall should be a center for intellectual life, that it should serve as a primary group affiliation of the student, and that it should assume responsibility for some of the major outcomes of collegiate education. All these imply having trained adults living in the dormitory or residence hall so they can organize definitely educational experiences and be available when students need conferences. Many persons qualified to do such things, however, find living in constant relationship with late adolescent students a wearing experience. Resident counselors or advisers discover that one or two years is enough before they wish to establish residences of their own. Even the Roman Catholic institutions, in which religious members might conceivably be happy to live in the residence hall, experience this problem. One hears sincere religious members saying they would prefer to live in the building created for members of the order rather than in close proximity to students. The alternative to finding adequately trained personnel has been to select house mothers from among faculty widows or somewhat elderly spinsters for whom maintaining a private residence would be a burden. Some of these house mothers have undoubtedly served an important role, and students think back pleasantly of having taken personal problems to an understanding, mature female. Neither by training nor inclination, however, are such people equipped to convert a residence hall into an integral part of the institution's educational program.

Another aspect of student personnel is student government. There has grown up the belief that students as emerging adults should be given considerable responsibility for themselves in the collegiate community, that self-management in college is sound training for self-management in the larger society. But with the exception of such outstanding examples as Antioch College, student government has consisted more in the form than in the substance of real government. Students are encouraged to organize, to form constitutions, to elect officers, and to discuss endlessly a variety of matters. Yet real government is impossible with the faculty or administration retaining the substance of power. A few institutions have recognized this and have made a formal grant of power to the student body for a specified period of time. By and large, however, the extent of student responsibility has not been made explicit, and students find themselves in the position of never knowing whether decisions will or will not be binding. Out of such indecision has come the tendency for student government to become preoccupied with the superficial and informal things of college life. Thus endless debates are held regarding a petition to the administration to abolish compulsory chapel, a recommendation that the school intensify school spirit, or the approval of methods by which students can earn or solicit funds for social activities.

It may be that this pattern is changing. In the years immediately following the publication of the Jacob Report on Student Values,[1] the National Student Association became more active, and small liberal arts colleges which had never been affiliated established relationships with it. Further, with a slowly awakening student interest in social and political problems in the late 1950's and early 1960's, have come more strident demands for student government to be given real responsibility. Whether or not this materializes or was just a temporary success sparked by sit-in demonstrations, freedom rides, and shame in comparison with the politically active European student, only time will answer.

Possibly the most thoroughly developed aspect of student personnel services has to do with the social life of students. From the mixers, rush parties and the like, characterizing orientation week, to the commencement week round of parties, smokers, reunions, the typical liberal arts college appears to consist of an endless array of social events. The reasons are obvious. In many of the small towns in which liberal arts colleges are located, readily available commercial entertainment is nonexistent. Further, young people of college age are very definitely seeking to learn to conduct themselves socially in a heterosexual adult society and are also seriously in search of mates. This is not an unfavorable objective for higher education. It is entirely appropriate for a young woman to use attendance at college as a means of achieving one of her important life goals. One may, however, be a little critical about the disproportionate emphasis socializing has assumed in such institutions. While it is probably a canard that excessive activity in social life prevents students from meeting their class obligations, it is still a fact that devoting ten to fifteen hours a week to organized social activities may be excessive when normal study outlay of time will rarely exceed ten hours a week for average students.

---

[1] Philip Jacob, *Changing Values in College* (New York: Harper & Brothers, 1957).

Another well-developed part of student personnel, especially in the church-related institutions, is the religious life of the campus. Although there is a slight tendency for colleges to abolish required chapel, considerable religious activity is still organized by officers of the institution. This may take the form of religious emphasis weeks, required attendance at chapel, vespers services, religious retreats, and in the more affluent colleges, the existence of a college chapel. In Roman Catholic institutions, particularly the liturgical ones, the décor of the buildings and classrooms is designed to intensify religious feeling and belief. There is an issue, however, which has nowhere been satisfactorily resolved. This is the extent to which the religious concerns of a college should be completely pervasive through the institution. If one argues they should be, the question then arises as to the difference between a Christian calculus and a non-Christian one, between Roman Catholic social science and Congregational social science. On the other hand the absence of this pervasiveness may result in perplexity for the student. To what extent do organized religious activities interfere with the student's personal freedom and the educational mission of the institution? Perhaps no other issue is so hotly debated on the campuses of religious affiliated liberal arts schools. Faculty members have been known to stop speaking to each other on the question of abolition of required church attendance.

The emphasis given social activities and religious affairs may be contrasted with that given to counseling and advising. Academic advising in the majority of liberal arts colleges is considered the province of the faculty, which probably is as it should be. The faculty, however, rarely is trained in the nuances of even the simple task of academic and vocational advising. It has been assumed that the possession of an advanced degree is sufficient qualification for a faculty member to advise students as to what they should take. Further, the load carried by faculty members in these small institutions prevents them from knowing the precise requirements for vocations, for graduate and professional study, and even, one must suspect, for graduation from their own institutions. Thus one is left with the conviction that advising, even on academic matters, is a hit-or-miss affair. If students happen to be in an institution in which almost every faculty member keeps abreast of developments in his own subject, reasonable advising can result. One has the feeling, however, that this happens more rarely than is desired. One can speculate that at least part of the enormous attrition rate in the small liberal arts colleges stems from students having received inadequate advice. They find it easier to drop out of school than to rectify the errors their advisers made.

Even less effective is the counseling service in which, ideally, trained individuals work with students on deeply embedded personal problems or seriously perplexing academic or vocational ones. Only the unusual liberal arts college feels it can afford to employ a full-time counselor. Yet if more colleges would do so, it is possible that some of the difficulties of attending a small college might be reduced. For instance, a college might appoint a well-trained counselor who would devote part of his time to helping students and the rest to the in-service training of the faculty in the objectives and techniques of advising.

Student health is another aspect of student personnel. The typical pattern is for the liberal arts college to insist upon a routine physical examination as a condition for admission, and an inoculation for smallpox and, more recently, for polio. Chest X-rays may be taken if the local tuberculosis unit is available. The college may maintain one room in a dormitory or several rooms as a health center with a registered or practical nurse on duty. It will arrange with a local physician to be available on call and to spend a number of hours each week in the dispensary. Students mildly ill thus can get limited medical attention and, if bed rest is prescribed, go to a residence hall or fraternity house. More serious illness requires outside medical care and perhaps admission to a local hospital. For some time the charges for more than limited medical attention were borne by students, but in recent years colleges have offered medical insurance to their students at moderate rates.

The provision of medical care in colleges is a difficult problem. The late adolescent group is possibly one of the healthiest age groups in society. The childhood diseases have been passed and the disintegrative diseases of adulthood have not yet commenced; hence, relatively inadequate medical facilities may exist for years in a college with no seeming hurt. But the traumatic diseases of adolescents, their debilitating diseases such as mononucleosis, and their mental health suggest that greater medical care is really needed. One gets the impression from visiting student personnel workers in residential colleges that the American undergraduate is, or is becoming, a pronounced hypochondriac, with many examples of students exchanging diagnoses as well as pills and other remedies. This hypochondriasis is undoubtedly related to the mental health of students and may be important enough to warrant increased expenditure for medical care.

Student aid, student scholarship, and student employment also are appropriately lodged within student personnel concerns. Quite likely a number of small liberal arts colleges could not fill their dormitories and classrooms were it not for rather elaborate scholarship programs. The tuition charges of liberal arts colleges are normally much higher than those of state institutions. Since the state institutions are equipped to provide greater variety of service, the competition can only be met by liberal awards of scholarships or grants in aid. This is not to say that such assistance is intrinsically wrong; it is to imply that many of the weaker liberal arts colleges are devoting a disproportionate amount of their incomes to scholarships, grants in aid, or payment for student employment. One could argue that the smaller liberal arts college might use some of its scholarship funds for increasing the salaries of faculty, and thus create a better institution that could compete on valid terms with the state-supported colleges or the more affluent liberal arts colleges. Furthermore, the basis for awarding scholarships will all too frequently not stand scrutiny. To the obviously restricting scholarships for particular classes of students (e.g., for Confederate heirs, for red-haired Baptists, and the like) are added scholarships for children of ministers or of educators, for athletes, and for musicians. Probably the ideal scholarship program would be a series of unrestricted scholarship grants which would be made on the basis of scholastic ability and demonstrated need. More liberal arts colleges should take advantage of the financial reporting service of the College Entrance Examination Board at Princeton, New Jersey. It collects financial information with the least amount of embarrassment to families who wish financial help for their children.

Several other activities need only be mentioned to have sketched in the dimensions of the student personnel effort found in liberal arts colleges. Alumni affairs are becoming increasingly significant as colleges seek additional sources of funds. As this happens, the alumni office slips from the student personnel organization to a position directly related to the president's office through his development program. The extracurricular clubs and activities are clearly student personnel in their orientation and seem to shift as the whole pattern of behavior of American college students shifts. For example, since World War II, the pattern of student exodus over the weekend has become prevalent. This means students are not nearly as available as they once were to participate in the preparation of yearbooks, in subject-matter clubs, and the like. The weakness lies in the fact that student personnel officers have not accepted the changes in the larger society, and try to keep alive student activities which are really moribund. There is an ambivalence here. Student personnel workers want to keep student activities going, hence are constantly seeking to enlist faculty support as sponsors; yet the significance of the activity is directly related to whether or not there is an interested faculty person to sponsor it and a truly interested group of students who want the activity. One could urge that each student generation should be given great freedom to decide what organized activities they believe are valuable and what ones they would like to see disappear. It is difficult for a student personnel worker, interested in creating programs, to assume this permissive attitude, yet it may well be the healthiest one possible. This point appears to be gaining significance. While the evidence is not yet clear, one gets the impression that college students in this age of sputnik, intellectual rigor, and increasing academic emphasis may be less interested in organized activities than they were at other periods in history. If this is so, the activity phase of the student personnel effort might well be de-emphasized.

In view of these complexities, it is perhaps time for even the smallest liberal arts college to review its efforts, including its philosophy in creating a more stable structure for its student personnel services. Such a review must necessarily resolve a number of issues.

First is clearly that of the degree of support the college is willing to give to its personnel activities. An institution which has devoted a considerable sum to an elaborate student personnel program has done so on the ground that students' out-of-class life is of equal educational significance with the in-class life. It has assumed that students can learn as many needed skills in the context of a residence hall as they can in the context of any particular subject. Not all institutions will arrive at this answer. Another might elect to place its principal resources into the curriculum and allow student personnel activities to grow naturally out of those concerns.

Thus the institution needs to decide how elaborate a student personnel program it wishes to mount. In doing so, it must face honestly the fact that whatever activities it sponsors will be less than adequate unless they are appropriately supported financially. One of the biggest weaknesses of student personnel effort in the smaller liberal arts college has been that responsibility was assigned to someone who already had a full-time position. When this happens, the individual assigned the extra work must make choices himself. Either his class work or the student personnel commitment may suffer. As a general rule, it would be better for a college not to adopt an activity unless it saw clearly available the resources to support it. Intensive counseling can help, but a college is more honest with itself and with its prospective students if it does not even offer intensive counseling unless it stands ready to have a trained full-time counselor do the work.

A second issue involves the stance of the college regarding the regulation of student behavior, including political behavior. Some institutions allow students virtually the complete freedom given an adult in American society, and do so successfully. Others allow students complete decision about mode of dress, men and women visiting each other in dormitory rooms, use of alcohol, travel to and from the campus, and political expression. Still others successfully operate while prescribing in considerable detail all these matters and laying down definite regulations regarding contacts between the sexes, use of automobiles, hours of checking in and out of dormitories, and participation in convocations. Very likely, an institution may adopt virtually any policy regarding regulation of student conduct it desires and still have a contented, effective student body, so long as the policy is made clear and the students understand it even before they attend the institution. The colleges where considerable unrest is found are those that are ambivalent about student conduct. Those which say students are responsible for their own behavior, but in which administrative officers prescribe how students shall dress, are likely to have a low student morale. The college which says "conscience is an individual concern," but insists on participation in denominational religious exercises, is open to criticism. Another which attempts to develop a stance regarding student conduct that is at variance with the stance of its constituency is also heading for trouble. Thus a college sponsored by a fundamentalist religious group which attracts students only from that religious group and at the same time makes its requirements clear before admissions, can succeed remarkably well. Wheaton College in Wheaton, Illinois, has a set of regulations regarding student conduct which very probably would terrorize students of a state institution, yet its student body constantly demonstrates high academic achievement and high esprit de corps. It is the liberal arts college that prescribes for students more, or less, than its constituency normally does, which creates the problems.

A third issue that must be resolved is the relationship of student personnel activities to the curricular concerns of the institution. This issue really goes to the intrinsic character of the institution. If the college believes that the curriculum or the academic mission is paramount, then it views all student personnel activities as supportive or reinforcing of the primary role of the college. If it makes explicit to student personnel workers that their role must always be subordinate to the academic, few problems will arise. If, however, the institution says it values the academic above all other activities, but fails to select student personnel workers who can agree to this, dislocations will happen.

On many campuses student personnel workers have been the butt of bitter criticism from the academic side. One suspects that a good part of this criticism has come about because student personnel workers were seen assuming equal importance with the curricular officers of the college. Every college should make its position clear on this point. It may very well hold that class work and extra-class work are equally important; so long as the academic staff understand this, problems do not arise. If, however, faculty members recruited from the graduate training institution with one image of what a college should be, are placed in a college that makes social clubs, student government, and residence-hall living equal in importance to history, English, or mathematics, faculty bitterness is sure to emerge.

Still another issue involves the general orientation of the whole student personnel program. It may be designed primarily to further the religious or moral concerns of the college. Or it may be more socially oriented, its workers preoccupied with student activities. Or it may be aimed principally at getting students into the college, overseeing their progress, and moving them out smoothly. Still another focus could be counseling and advising, the main preoccupation being to deal with the students' personal problems if they seem to interfere with achievement of institutional goals. Obviously, no program will admit to being exclusively concerned with any one of these focuses. Since the institution will likely have limited resources, it might better concentrate on one of these than try to do all with equal vigor.

All these issues must be resolved in the light of the experience of individual institutions. Their resolution may be facilitated by adherence to some general theory of student personnel work, based on a series of postulates. One is that the central purpose of an institution of higher learning is intellectual, cognitive, and academic. All else in it is designed to support its central purpose. To this postulate many may take exception. It should be recalled, however, that society meets the needs of its members through social institutions, each having primary responsibility for some portion of societal requirement. The institution may collaborate with others or duplicate a portion of another's responsibility, yet not violate its primary obligation. The church in American society provides recreational facilities for its members, assumes some leadership in the resolution of social problems, and through its sponsored schools offer education for the young. Yet none of these activities is its primary function, which is to mediate between the individual and the unsolved mysteries of human life, between him and some form of deity. The army maintains churches and recreational centers and does constructive work such as flood control, yet its primary societal responsibility is protection of the nation. The list could be extended. The American college or university does fulfill many duties. It provides spectator sports and thus is in the entertainment business. It provides housing, hospital care, recreational facilities, and food service. Each of these, however, should be attempted only if the activity supports or reinforces the fundamental purpose of the institution.

Similarly one can raise questions about the propriety of a college using funds for the spectator sport of football. One can approve of a counseling program that attempts to remove superficial personality barriers to an individual's achievement of intellectual objectives, while disapproving of a counseling operation that attempts prolonged psychotherapy and reconstruction of personality. One can support modest recreational efforts in connection with residence halls, yet reject the attempt of residence-hall officials to elevate such activities to the status of academic courses.

A second postulate is that the real needs of American college students are in the process of fundamental change and that this change should govern the nature of student personnel services. In the nineteenth century America represented essentially a rural or small-town society from which only the children of the relatively wellborn attended college. There is some evidence that the four years at college was really looked upon by parents as a reasonable waiting period before their children should start to work. The primary group relationships of a paternalistic family and small-town church and community provided the necessary stability for personality growth of young people. College could be and was a period of wild rebellion and gay living. It is out of this milieu that the college life, effectively but fictitiously portrayed by Dink Stover at Yale, emerged. Many of the attributes of the present-day student personnel movement seem to have been created to channelize those wilder, more exuberant spirits of an earlier time. The fraternity system, bane of all student personnel officers—some of whom very likely were independents themselves—is a product of the nineteenth century. Its pertinency for the contemporary student is at least open to question.

There is growing evidence that today's American student is much more interested in forming small, primary group relationships on a campus than in joining the larger groups such as fraternities, sororities, social clubs, and similar organizations. Despite critics' judgments, the American college student is much more serious-minded about his goals and about the role a college education is to play in achieving them. Among other reasons, the present college generation represents a much wider segment of American society, many of whom are using collegiate education as a means of moving up socially.

While the full intensity of the changes taking place in the needs of students has yet to be understood, enough is known to suggest that a number of student personnel activities should be brought seriously into question. Further, enough is known to suggest to student personnel officers that the course of wisdom would be to study emerging student needs and let their programs evolve naturally from those. To make this more specific, intercollegiate athletics may well be a vanishing phenomenon. To perpetuate it may be a useless waste of institutional funds. Student clubs and social groups may be superfluous when student interest is shifting toward curricular matters. Officers of some of the new institutions might wait several years before crystallizing a student personnel program until they see the direction of student interests. The same injunction could be issued to private liberal arts colleges of longer history.

A third postulate is that students need adult contact and adult advice, but not too much. Perhaps the greatest need of the present college student is to develop a relationship with some professional person in college who is available when the student wants him, but who restrains himself from prying when the student wishes solitude. This need has become pronounced in part because of the changing complexion of family relationships. When fathers lived and worked close to the home, they were ideal persons with whom young people could identify. The contemporary pattern of fathers going away from home each day removes this necessary model. An adviser sensitive to this need of students may come to be the most important student personnel officer an institution can have. Stephens College in Columbia, Missouri, has developed a number of programs in higher education, probably the most significant of which is its adviser system. Under it each student can establish intimate relationships with one faculty person. From the stability of this relationship, the student can explore comfortably all aspects of the curriculum.

A fourth postulate is that automation can and should do much of what is now done by student personnel workers. The scheduling of classes and making of decisions for admission or suspension can be accomplished by machines. Even the smallest liberal arts college can contract with centers for the tabulation of data for much of this work. Further, much of the routine instructing of students in the ways of college life and in methods of study can be more efficiently handled by programmed instruction. One institution which for years offered a sub-collegiate course in mathematics for students deficient in those skills abolished the course in 1961. Deficient students were told to secure a programmed course in algebra and trigonometry and to work through it. A graduate student was made available in the event the student ran into difficulty, but the responsibility for improvement rested completely with the student. One can foresee that much of the remedial work now being done by student personnel officers can be taken over by some form of automated teaching.

A fifth postulate is that special kinds of people need to be used in the student personnel program. First of all, they should be trained either as part of their graduate work or as a result of a definite program of in-service training conducted by the institution. Very likely the small liberal arts college will be unable to recruit persons for each of its student personnel positions who have had relevant graduate training. At least one of the positions, however, could be so filled, with the understanding that the person selected would also be responsible for the in-service training of other workers.

In addition to training, student personnel workers, perhaps even more than other workers with young people, need to understand their own motivations. This is particularly important for those entering such a position as dean of students. By the nature of the post, a great deal of control of student behavior is possible. An institution appointing a dean of students might well inquire why he wishes to be in a position in which he can regulate such things as student dress, conduct, or even standards of taste. Such control, properly exercised, is probably necessary; but it can become repressive and restrictive in the hands of a person compulsively in need to control others. It can also be oppressive in the hands of one who believes his own standards of personal conduct are the right ones for all people. Similar questioning can be raised about those who become counselors. It may be true that some of the more effective counselors are those who became interested in counseling as they worked through rather deep-seated personal problems themselves. But the appointing institution needs to find out whether those problems have indeed been solved, or the counselor is inclined to use students in solving his own deeply embedded difficulties.

Lastly, those in student personnel need to possess characteristics that will earn respect of faculty and students alike. Student personnel workers have frequently attracted the irritation of the faculty, partly through their own errors and partly through lack of understanding on the part of teachers. One dean of students forever made himself suspect with the scientifically oriented members of the faculty by an initial speech in which he argued that the purpose of education was to break the normal curve of distribution. Another counselor virtually wrecked the student personnel program by excessive use of Freudian jargon. Perhaps it is unfair, but one can argue that student personnel workers need even higher respectability than other officers of the institution.

A sixth postulate in this theory of student personnel work is that more precise information about students is available and should be collected. It is sometimes amazing to note the kinds of decisions made about students or of advice given them in the absence of relevant or correct information. Students are advised to take a lighter load as the solution to an academic difficulty, without any basis in fact that this is an appropriate course of action. They are told that taking remedial work will help them acquire the tools they will need for subsequent upper level college work, without verifiable knowledge that this normally will happen. They are admitted to or rejected from a college too frequently on the subjective judgment of a high school principal, in spite of the very real possibility that personality assessment by high school counselors may be completely ineffective as predictors of academic success.

It is currently possible for colleges to bring together in one place a great deal of available information, not only about the student body collectively, but about individual students. The idea of a longitudinal study has relevance here. By this is meant the systematic accumulation of such things as high school records, test data, curricular choices, advisers' recommendations, and actions taken concerning a student during his collegiate career. Many of these data are already available, but typically have not been brought together in one place so that a complete pattern can be viewed. Once they are assembled in some easy-to-assimilate form, much more accurate generalizations are possible. Private liberal arts colleges could join with the publicly supported educational system within a state to insure a uniform system of record keeping and reporting for all students from elementary schools through graduate or professional schools. The Educational Testing Service and the State of Georgia have provided such a plan. Given the developments in electronic data processing, this is a distinct possibility for other states.

A seventh postulate is that the student personnel effort for a small privately supported liberal arts college should have distinctive characteristics not found in larger institutions. The liberal arts college being primarily residential, it might very well link its entire student personnel effort to this residential feature. Such colleges are normally small, ranging from 500 to 1,000 students. This smallness poses distinct problems and yet offers distinct solutions. It is quite possible that all members of a faculty in a small institution could be given considerable training to equip them to serve as advisers or counselors. Such a solution obviously would be inappropriate in a large institution.

An eighth postulate is that the administration of the student personnel program should always be subordinate to the academic program of the institution. There has grown up the recommendation from student personnel groups that the dean of student affairs should have equal status with the academic dean and the vice president for business and finance. From this has stemmed a hyperactive student personnel effort which may very well have mitigated against student achievement of the primary objectives of the institution. The student personnel activities obviously are important in the life of the institution, but the direction of them should be handled by an officer who while responsible to the president should always rank below the academic dean.

CHAPTER V

Administration: Leadership or Laissez-Faire

American collegiate education is different from English and European education in many respects, not the least important of which is the role played by administration. The faculties of Continental institutions follow the pattern of the medieval university and retain much of the control and direction of their own affairs. Heads of institutions are regarded as executives of the wishes of the faculty, and typically see themselves as serving but a short time as rector, chancellor, or president before returning to the more rewarding task of teaching and research. American colleges and universities, while owing much to the medieval tradition, derive their typical structure from the examples of the church, army, or corporation. Their chief officers are granted, by law, the complete direction of the organization and they exercise these powers. Indeed, American collegiate education is so administrator-oriented that there is a tendency for such persons to regard faculty members as nothing more than employees who happen to be skilled in one form of labor. There is some truth in the observation that many deans and presidents are inclined to see the professoriate as consisting of aspiring deans and presidents, who didn't make the grade. At least there is a strong tendency for persons who have once shifted to administration to remain there throughout the rest of their professional careers.

The small, privately supported liberal arts college normally has a relatively simple administrative structure. The president is the chief executive officer of the institution, responsible to a governing board which is the legal agency controlling the entire institution. The power and responsibility of the president within the policies of his board of trustees are legally quite complete. He is charged with employing assistants and officers of instruction. He is responsible for the properties and finances of the institution; he is supposed to develop programs to achieve the purposes of the institution and almost generally is expected to secure the bulk of the resources necessary to put these programs into effect. Historically, the president has been the primary officer of a college. In the nineteenth century he frequently was the sole officer of administration as well as one of the principal teachers.

As even the smallest institutions became more complex, the president found it necessary to subdivide his responsibilities and ask other individuals to assist him. Since maintaining academic records, placing students into appropriate classes, and certifying those for graduation, expulsion, or other change of status were probably the most burdensome and time-consuming tasks of the president, his first assistant was usually a registrar. This officer frequently was responsible for recruiting students, admitting them and scheduling them into classes, and for maintaining records for them and insuring that faculty members were available to meet classes. Most of these functions obtain at present. While there is some debate as to whether the registrar, with his admitting function, should also be responsible for recruitment of students, the main elements of his job have remained fairly constant. He has found it necessary in some of the larger liberal arts colleges to adopt newer, faster, more accurate methods of accounting for students and staff. He also has been called upon more and more frequently to provide statistical summaries to be used for college planning. His office gradually has solidified into a profession with its own national and regional organizations, its own journals, and its own place in the administrative hierarchy.

Out of the registrar's function has grown the office of dean of faculty or academic dean or dean of instruction. As the problems of class scheduling, course buildings, and academic advising grew, the registrar was unable to cope with them. The first academic deans were primarily officers attending to such details. Unfortunately, a number of academic deans in smaller liberal arts colleges still conceive of their task as essentially that of routine office workers. The office, however, is gradually being forced to expand its responsibilities. As the president becomes more and more preoccupied with securing financing for the institution and with the management of its fiscal and physical properties, he has had to relinquish some of his duties involving recruitment of faculty, curriculum building, and educational leadership. These have most logically fitted into the other duties of the academic dean, and generally go into his job description today. Thus, as a general rule, the academic dean currently will be responsible for the entire academic part of the program; he may have major responsibility concerning faculty personnel; he may be considered the second in command of the institution and not infrequently may be responsible for the office of the registrar, out of which his own office originally came.

The impact of the student personnel movement on American education, stemming as it did out of the concepts of progressive education and intensified psychological investigations, has resulted in a subdivision of the office of academic dean. Much counseling and advising of students concerns nonacademic matters. The control of students' out-of-class behavior seemed inappropriate for the chief officer of the academic program. The organization of extracurricular activities seemed to require talents different from those required for the organization of an academic program. Gradual awareness of these problems has resulted in the establishment of the office of dean of students or, a frequently found pattern, a dean of men and a dean of women, each responsible to the academic dean. Within the small liberal arts college this office has not generally developed to quite the level of institutionalization as the office of academic dean. In some of the relatively small institutions, the functions of a personnel dean are frequently assigned to someone who may be teaching half or even three-fourths of his time. There is, however, a detectable trend for the office to become clearly specified, for its duties to be outlined in detail, and for the holder of the office to become more and more independent of the academic dean. This tendency has been intensified by the efforts of associations of personnel workers who argue that the chief student personnel officer should have coequal status with the academic officer.

At present there are still twilight zones in which duties may be assigned one officer or the other, depending on the institution. At one college the registrar will be responsible to the academic dean, while at another he may be responsible to the dean of students. Academic advising may be solely the prerogative of the academic dean, jointly his affair and that of the student personnel dean, or the prerogative solely of the dean of students. The conduct of academic convocations, the preparation of honors lists, and other details may similarly be found under one officer or the other, or as joint responsibility. What the future of the office of dean of student personnel is to be is at this point conjectural. It continues to be sharply criticized by the academic staff yet keeps drifting toward greater autonomy.

The president of a small liberal arts college has the primary responsibility for financial support of the institution. Even though he spends a large proportion of his time on these activities, he is still unable to cope with fund raising and fund management at the same time. Further, as institutions expand their physical plants and their endowment funds, it has become important that some officer give full time to such matters. Thus, the office of president has been subdivided once again—this time in the form of a treasurer or a comptroller or a vice president for finance or a business manager. Such officers generally are responsible for the internal accounting, for properties of the institution, for assisting the president in the preparation of budgets, for supervision of the physical plant, and for management of the institution's portfolio of securities. In some institutions the chief fiscal officer is judged so important that he actually serves in place of the president when the president is out of town. A more frequently found pattern is for the chief fiscal officer to be responsible to the president, as is the academic dean. When the president is away, the two confer and make decisions by consensus or else await the return of the chief executive.

Normally responsible to the chief fiscal officer is the man in charge of maintenance of the physical plant, including the management of dormitories or food services and of police and fire units. Not infrequently he is designated assistant to the president for development.

It is in this development concern that the most recent of the major administrative officers has arisen. Particularly since World War II, private colleges have seen the necessity for constant drives to obtain money, both for normal operating expenses and for capital development. The president of the institution is intimately concerned with these matters, but has found that specialized knowledge and experience is necessary if he is to mount successful campaigns. He has, therefore, appointed an assistant, sometimes paid for out of operating budgets and sometimes out of separate funds, to develop long-term campaigns or special campaigns for designated projects, to secure up-to-date information about fund raising, and to assist the president generally in this important matter. In some institutions, the development officer is given a title such as vice president, to grant him the necessary status to represent the institution before large and influential prospective donors.

In addition to these principal officers, a number of minor administrative posts are beginning to appear in even the smallest colleges. As was true with some of the other positions, these may be held by individuals who are also teaching or doing other duties for the institution. As the college grows in size and complexity, however, these offices become more and more separate. A director of a news bureau, a public relations officer, or a press officer is one example. He normally reports directly to the president, since the president is so directly concerned with the image the institution presents to its various publics. As a college assumes more responsibility for its students, even after graduation, and as it looks to its alumni for support and assistance in the future, an alumni secretary has become essential. He helps the college maintain alumni clubs, publishes bulletins, magazines, and brochures to alumni groups, and in general maintains contact with graduates. He may be salaried by the college or by the alumni group.

Some institutions rely so heavily on student tuition as a financial base that the director of admissions is considered a chief administrative officer. He, either alone or through a staff of field workers, must identify those students who can likely profit from the program the college has to offer.

A number of the institutions having quite close relationships with a sponsoring church may very well have a director of religious activities, a chaplain or a dean of religion as part of the administrative staff. This office is even found on a few campuses with no direct tie with any established church. Generally, the chief religious officer serves as a religious adviser for students, conducts officially prescribed religious activities, sponsors special religious efforts such as a religious emphasis week, and sometimes assists the president in his relationships with the churches comprising the constituency of the college.

Several other minor administrative offices are beginning to emerge on the campuses of small liberal arts colleges. The president may employ a part-time educational consultant. He may contract with one of the larger consulting firms on college development. There may be a specific office in charge of testing. A few institutions have even created an office of institutional research, although this is a luxury few of the smaller schools have felt they could afford. They are more likely to afford some person responsible for audio-visual materials.

Separate mention must be made of the librarian. Almost every catalogue of a liberal arts college states that the library is the real heart of the institution. Thus, it would seem that the librarian or director of libraries as custodian of this central activity might logically be one of the chief aids to the president. Generally he is not. In most cases his salary is below that of other officers with comparable responsibilities. Not infrequently he has no direct access to the president and may sometimes be considered roughly equal to heads of the relatively small departments characteristic of the smaller liberal arts college. While librarians generally deplore this situation, and are making efforts to rectify it, tendencies toward greater stature for the librarian do not seem to be moving rapidly.

Below this level of principal administrative officers are those individuals charged with supervising the separate academic units on the campus. These consist of departmental heads or chairmen, divisional heads, directors, or chairmen, and the directors of a number of specialized services such as counseling, remedial services, physical education, and the like. Since the units these persons supervise are frequently small, one has a feeling that perhaps administrative titles have been used to reward faculty members, sometimes in lieu of adequate salaries.

These various administrative offices have come into existence in response to specific problems faced by emerging liberal arts colleges. The nature of these problems is so clearly implied by the administrative duties discussed as to need no further analysis. A number of other problems involving administration do, however, need to be made explicit.

Possibly the most serious lack in the privately supported liberal arts college today is educational leadership. The president, who is legally responsible, is so preoccupied with management matters as to be unable to keep abreast of educational thinking, much less translate it into educational action. The academic dean, frequently one of the weakest links in the administrative chain, has too generally been an older respected teacher, given the post of dean in his declining years. This abdication of the leadership role has meant that the faculty itself carried on the educational program too generally along lines demanded by tradition. Unless this problem of leadership can be solved, in view of the contemporary condition of rapid social change, the privately supported liberal arts college may very well find itself outclassed by the state supported institutions and unable to maintain itself as an educational force.

A second critical problem is the inability of some of the less affluent institutions to provide even modest personnel and equipment for effective administration. There is something incongruous in a liberal arts college with a physical plant worth five to ten millions of dollars and an operating budget of a million dollars in which the chief educational officer painfully inscribes correspondence in longhand to be transcribed by a part-time student secretary. The inability of weaker institutions to rent or purchase necessary equipment for treatment of data again places unnecessary drain on human beings who might be using their energies for creative thought about the institution. The necessity to assign major administrative tasks to part-time people virtually assures the smaller liberal arts colleges of mediocre teaching and mediocre administration. This inability of the small institution to appoint full-time officers to maintain essential administrative functions has led some critics to remark that almost invariably, in spite of the plethora of titles, the smaller liberal arts college is underadministered.

Another problem, only dimly perceived at the present, is that of maintaining the continuity of the administration of the liberal arts college. For years college presidents had relatively brief tenures—an average of something over four years. Later, according to a study by William K. Seldon, the tenure of presidents was found to have increased markedly to approximately eight years. One has the feeling, however, that the continuity which should be transmitted through the office of the academic dean is still lacking. Deans change office as frequently as presidents. Further, it seems that colleges have never satisfactorily solved the problems of succession. If an institution has a strong president who retains office for a long time, he is almost invariably followed by a weak president at the mercy of a resurgent faculty. One can almost lay it down as an axiom that different kinds of presidents will be found at different periods in the institution's history. Each of these shifts in orientation results in considerable loss of educational momentum on the part of the faculty and the entire organization.

A fourth problem is that of the administration of the separate academic units of the college. The Germanic research tradition in American scholarship has elevated the subject department to a position of primacy, and possibly departments are essential in large, complicated universities. However, a one- or two-person department in a thirty- or forty-person faculty seems somewhat ridiculous. The group is not large enough to provide what David Riesman has called a critical mass of people, large enough to insure mutual intellectual stimulation. Further, it is not large enough to have a budget big enough to be administered. Neither is it large enough to involve any real supervision of personnel. It would seem that some form of divisional structure in which people of related subjects are brought together would be logical. The problem, however, has been to create a structure which could have real power and influence and which could command the loyalties of faculty members in them. For some inexplicable reason, divisions in even those colleges maintaining them have not proved effective. It may be that some other kind of administrative organization is necessary for the academic units of the small liberal arts college. Possibly all units could be abolished, with the responsibilities of departments re-assumed by the academic dean. This does not appear to be a likely solution. Parkinson's Law probably applies as well to the small liberal arts college as it does to the business community. Possibly, special organizations to be changed relatively frequently, or a divisional structure based on adequate delegation of power may, after all, be the answer.

Still another problem the liberal arts college must face is to find administrative means to meet the emerging needs of colleges in the last half of the twentieth century. The growing relationships of colleges to the federal government, as higher education is more and more viewed as an instrument of national policy, is one such need. The necessity for accurate institutional planning for the decades ahead, when even the new vocations which will attract people are unknown, is another. The surging demand of adults for education to equip them for greater longevity is still another, as is the means for utilizing modern technology for instructional purposes. The potentialities of television, of closed circuit radio, of teaching machines, of study abroad all require excellent administration if they are to be effectively utilized. Yet the small liberal arts college has not evolved ways of providing the requisite administration. One can speculate on the frustration of a liberal arts college president or dean attending educational meetings, and hearing of the dramatic changes possible through newer media of instruction, which he knows full well he cannot utilize because he lacks the administrative time properly to relate faculty energies to them.

Since a growing number of Roman Catholic institutions are classified as liberal arts colleges, one peculiar administrative problem of theirs must be mentioned. Normally Roman Catholic colleges are conducted by one of the orders. These are governed by canon law which prescribes rigidly the relationships between members. The order of St. Benedict may be taken as an example, in which the head of the order is the supreme authority with manifold responsibilities for the lives of the members and for the management of far-flung enterprises. He or she is limited to the six years authorized by canon law. Thus, if the institution makes the head of the chapter the president of the institution as well, an enforced discontinuity is inevitable. If the institution divorces the role of president from that of the head of the chapter, a different problem emerges. All members of the order are considered equal under the paternalistic rule of the abbot, the mother superior, or the general. Thus, the president, supposedly the chief executive officer of the institution, would be subordinate to another member of the order and equal to all faculty members and other administrative officers. Many solutions have been suggested to this problem, an ingenious one being to vest the head of the chapter with the presidency and change presidents according to the time of canon law, but appoint a non-Roman Catholic vice president as the chief educational leader of the institution. At any rate, this matter of administrative continuity and administrative relationship within the Roman Catholic schools needs resolution.

Some solutions to administrative problems may be suggested by probing in depth several critical administrative relationships. The first of these involves the relationship between the president and the academic dean. The president of a college, as the legal executive officer of the board of control, actually conducts the institution. He is expected to preserve its sense of direction and unity, to identify himself with the future and fortunes of his school, and to direct his most stringent efforts to improve both. While professors may pay scant attention to the catalogue, the president is expected to know and believe everything it says. Then he is expected to interpret his institution to the various publics which impinge on the college. The effectiveness of the institution can be assured only when interested people know and agree with its goals. It is the president's task to see that they do. As the executive of the board of control, he is expected to employ such persons as are necessary for the functioning of the college and to coordinate their efforts to secure maximum achievement. While he may delegate responsibility and authority, ultimately he is the responsible person and must account to his board for every action taken in his name. Obviously, to secure harmony in working toward institutional goals, he is expected to provide leadership to his faculty and to his administrative assistants. While it is subsumed under a more general duty, the task of fund raising is so crucial as to warrant mention as a separate responsibility. The president is expected to secure whatever funds are necessary for the conduct of his program.

Since the primary business of the college is education and research, the subordinate most closely associated with those activities has come to hold a unique relationship to the president and to the institution. The dean of the college, or dean of faculty, or academic dean, typically is expected to carry out one or all of these duties:

1. Direct the educational activities of the college
2. Act as chief adviser to the president in matters of college policy, particularly in academic affairs
3. Formulate educational policies and present them to the president and faculty for consideration
4. Direct the attention of faculty members to changing educational thought and practice, particularly as they affect higher education
5. Transmit to the president the budget recommendations for academic activities, after details have been worked out with department heads
6. Make reports relating to the work of the college
7. Supervise curriculums, courses and methods of instruction
8. Cooperate with heads of departments in the nomination of new members for the teaching staff, and make suggestions to the president regarding the promotion, demotion, or dismissal of members of the faculty

9. Assist in the recruiting of students
10. Classify students and assign them to classes
11. Study the progress and academic welfare of students
12. Serve as chief disciplinary officer of the college
13. Represent the college at meetings of educational institutions

On the face of these two specifications—education and research—there would seem to be no major difficulties in effecting a division of labor or a sharing of responsibilities between the chief administrative officer and his chief assistant. But, because both offices are still in transition, major dislocations are frequent.

Several bars to effective shared responsibility between the president and dean are related to the collegiate organizational structure. The dean has come to occupy a line and a staff relationship. As adviser to the president on academic matters and on faculty affairs, he is a staff officer, and as such has no decision-making power. It is his duty to obtain full information about a problem, on the basis of which the president can make his decision. But since presidents are absent a great deal and since deans are so intimately involved in the on-going activities of the institution, the dean has also been granted some line authority. In this role he stands between the president and the heads of departments or divisions. The difficulty of this situation stems from the fact that in any organization line and staff functions are hard to blend. The kind of mentality that can accumulate facts and then stand by and see someone else use them is different from the kind that wants to make decisions. In education the matter is further complicated by the fact that few people are aware of when the line role and when the staff role should obtain. Professors frequently feel justified in dealing directly with the president about matters which are within the line responsibility of the dean.

This complexity is made more significant by the fact that there does exist a considerable tradition of conflict between faculty and administration. Faculties are intent on their own specialties and conservative of time-honored values. Presidents, as administrators, are vehicles of social change, hence a threat to professors. Professors in a sense represent the medieval tradition of the university as a community of self-regulating scholars, while the president represents the church or military tradition of unitary control directed toward social change. The dean is injected into this situation of conflict with no clear guidelines to govern his conduct. As an appointee of the president, he is clearly of the administrative side, yet in all likelihood he has come from many years of teaching and research service and shares many of its sentiments. Further, any conflict, whether latent or manifest, is tension-creating and tension does not permit fullest cooperation and sharing of confidence and of responsibility. In colleges in which both the president and faculty are at least covertly suspicious of the motives of the other, a free blending of ideas with another agency is difficult for each to accomplish. The reality of this dilemma facing deans is evidenced by the decision individual deans have made. Most have openly joined the president and are inclined to think of themselves as part of the administration. A few have moved in the other direction and have continued to think of themselves as spokesmen for the faculty in representations to the president.

A third factor inherent in the organization of colleges is the legal reality of the board as the final agency of control. The institution is in the hands of a group of men who employ the president as their legal representative. Any division of responsibility or of authority with a dean is done at the will of the president and can legally be altered at his will. This unilateral relationship strongly mitigates against a genuine sharing of responsibility. In any final analysis, the president must make a decision. In event a strong president and an equally strong dean each believed himself to be right and the other wrong, the final decision rests with the president. It is true that this has been circumvented, especially in situations where a dean has exercised extralegal pressure on a board of control. Typically, however, the president's will prevails, and this affects the freedom of interaction between the dean and his chief.

One should not infer that the relationships between the dean and president are always troubled. One can visit many institutions in which the relationship is most cordial, where many of these difficulties have been overcome by any of a variety of means. The difficulties do, however, seem of sufficient significance and frequency to warrant sincere attempts of college administrators to rectify them. As with any other complicated human endeavor, there is no panacea, but there are a few techniques or approaches or principles which seem to have been effective in overcoming some of these problems.

Relatively early in a dean-president relationship, these men should have a serious, protracted discussion of their mutual self-images. A frank exchange of views as to what is expected of the other might accomplish wonders in removing major misconceptions. Since the dean is concerned with the most important aspect of college work—the academic—he should have a primary position among the advisers of the president. He might well be given the function, if not the title, of provost or vice president, with the clear understanding that during the absence of the president he acts in his place.

Both the president and dean have the obligation to work for the professionalization of the role of college administrator. Both men should search the literature of personnel management and educational management to find out more about the processes of administration. The whole tradition in American education is such that persons once committed to administration tend to remain there. What more fitting than that these men become truly professional in the activities that will engage their energies during their most creative years.

The dean-president relationship is such in certain situations that the only solution is to break off the relationship. A backdoor should always be provided so that in event a dean and president just cannot get along together, the dean can be relieved of administrative duties, without involving loss of face or undue financial loss. This does not argue that a dean could not be relieved for general incompetence and should suffer financial loss as a result of it. It does say that there are many situations in which men of good will just cannot get along. A person should not be asked to sacrifice himself because of divergence of opinion, or to do the more objectionable thing of sacrificing his considered opinions just for the sake of retaining office.

A second administrative problem involves the relationships of the president and faculty with the board of trustees. The board is the legal controlling body for the institution, yet it should exercise this power in only limited ways. Someone has remarked that the primary obligation of a board of trustees is to employ a president and thereafter approve the president's programs so long as he continues to enjoy the confidence of the board. This is probably too extreme a position. Perhaps a more prudent relationship can be revealed in a series of prescriptions.

1. The board of trustees must employ a president and should serve as an advising group for whatever programs the president feels justified in recommending. The board may raise questions, seek further information and even recommend deferring a particular action. A president might well feel he had lost his effectiveness if his board of trustees acts counter to his recommendations more than a few times.

2. The board exercises its authority as a corporate body. No individual board member should assume the prerogative of appointing a president, criticizing an officer of the institution, or seeking particular changes in institutional policy. A member of the board of trustees is simply another individual with respect to the concerns of the college, except when his voice is joined to that of his colleagues in an official decision.

3. The board makes its decisions known to and felt by the president and the president alone. It should not feel entitled to call in any other member of the administration or faculty on any question except at the specific information of the president of the institution. Occasionally, a board may have the chief fiscal officer as an ex officio member to serve as treasurer for the board. This relationship, while it has advantages, is hazardous and must be watched carefully.

4. The board, whether it be self-perpetuating or elected, is intended to reflect the beliefs of its supporting constituency. As such, it has an obligation to determine the views of that constituency and to interpret these to the college administration. As a corollary, it should view itself as a screen to protect the administration of the college from isolated actions by members of a constituency. Thus, the board should be entitled to receive complaints from ministers of supporting churches, should place these complaints in perspective, and then discuss the matter with the president of the college.

5. The board should take an active interest not only in the financial affairs of the college and the selection of the president, but also in curricular and educational matters. It should, however, never assume professional competency in such concern. It should stand ready on the request of the president to give laymen's reactions to educational problems, but should not presume to place itself above its professional employees in deciding the merits of a particular educational question. There are two major errors which boards often commit in this regard. The first is to ignore educational matters completely. There is rarely a president who hasn't heard a board member say, "I will attend the meeting for the business portion. I'll have to leave before you get to the educational part." The other

error is for the board to attempt to become operational about educational questions. A middle course is what is needed.

A last administrative problem to be presented in this attempt to understand the administrative process in a small liberal arts college concerns faculty participation and administrative responsibility. There is, perhaps, more time lost on college campuses by the attempt of faculty committees to serve as administrative agencies than for any other single reason. Yet the opposite end of the continuum is equally undesirable. Faculty members are professional people who rightly feel that they should have some clear voice in their professional destinies and in the use of their professional talents. They are not employees of the president but are simply professional colleagues working in a different capacity. While there can be no perfect resolution, perhaps the matter of faculty and administrative responsibilities can be improved by following several principles:

1. Faculty members, within powers granted them by the governing board, should be policy-making rather than administrative groups. In general, the board of trustees should clearly grant the faculty power to set policy regarding the curriculum, instructional methods, standards of admission and graduation, and screening of professional colleagues. This grant of power should not, however, be extended to actual administration of these matters. The faculty should decide on the general subjects to be included in the curriculum. But the administration, consisting here of the dean and president and divisional head, must decide what resources the institution can put into the project. The faculty can certainly decide on the general qualifications of people to be appointed to new positions, but should not assume the final appointing authority, which rests with the administrative officer. An interesting device for new appointments is for the faculty to suggest four or five candidates, any of whom would be satisfactory, the final choice left to the administrative officer. In this connection it should be remembered that the tyranny of an autocratic administrator is fully equalled by the tyranny of an irresponsible faculty committee seeking to exercise administrative power.

2. The faculty should enjoy academic freedom together with the freedom exercised by all people in American society. This freedom, however, must be exercised appropriately. When it is, the administration is bound to support its faculty. When it is not, the administration must undertake to use its proper prerogatives. Every faculty member has the freedom to speak the truth as he sees it

concerning those subjects about which he is professionally competent. When he seeks to use his professorial position as a platform from which to speak about things for which he has only a layman's knowledge, he is open to criticism.

3. The faculty member's relationships with the institution and with the administration should be governed by principles of relevancy. A faculty member is a professional person who professes a certain subject. So long as he does so competently, as appraised by his professional colleagues, he should be free from criticism or sanction from his administrative superiors. A teacher being considered for faculty appointment should be judged on relevant professional criteria only. Thus, an administration has no ethical right to interview a candidate's wife as being a relevant consideration in the appointment. If a candidate's wife proves to be a charming contribution to the college community, this is an unearned increment. If she does not, but her husband continues to be an effective faculty member, even the most shrewish wife is no excuse for administrative interference with faculty freedom. If a wife interferes with her husband's work, that will be judged when the work itself is appraised.

In addition to the principles involved in the specific problems of the relationships between the dean and president, the divisional organization, the relationships with boards of trustees and the problem of faculty responsibility, several transcendent principles or postulates may be advanced. Some of these, it must be admitted, need to be further tried in practice. They appear at this point, however, to be warrantable assertions. As the pressures of numbers, the effects of an inflationary economy, and the needs for new physical plants have been felt, there has been a series of recommendations and efforts to bring better business management techniques into collegiate administration. There has been the attempt to use standardized accounting procedures, more effective ways of utilizing space, and more efficient means of record keeping. This tendency has been resisted in some institutions on the ground that education is not really susceptible to business and management procedures. Education, it is argued, is an intangible thing for which there can never be the clear-cut criterion of success such as is served for business by a profit and loss statement. And faculty effort is such a spontaneous sort of creativity that faculty work loads cannot be judged in the same way work loads are for business and industry.

This first postulate affirms that, criticisms and resistances to the contrary, it is very probable that truly effective business or managerial procedures are really good educational procedures. A slight corollary should be added that if effective management is not necessarily good education, at least it is not antithetical to good education. There is no existing evidence to support a concentration of instructional hours in the prime morning periods of from 9:00 to 12:00, nor is there evidence that every-other-day scheduling of courses is pedagogically better than asymmetrical scheduling of courses during the week. Effective management, spreading the use of instructional space throughout the day and perhaps into the evening hours, thus is feasible. There is no real evidence that a highly diversified curriculum is educationally defensible, yet faculties have been notoriously hard to persuade to reduce course offerings. The pressures of strict cost accounting, which can demonstrate the extravagance of a large number of small classes, may be a wise way of forcing the curriculum within reasonable boundaries. There is no valid reason to suppose that the college teacher is, by the nature of his work, any more entitled to be remiss in administrative details such as getting in reports, grades, and the like than is any other person. Since, by and large, college teachers drift into their profession toward the later part of their undergraduate careers, there would not seem to be any personality characteristics really suggestive of poor administration. Indeed, if the college professor is assumed to be scholarly, one might even expect more precision in routine administrative matters than would be found in other complicated organizations. It might be well for the chief administrative officers of the liberal arts colleges to insist upon more precise administrative effort on the part of faculties, and this could probably be done without diminishing professors' effectiveness as teachers or scholars.

Obviously, if there were a stark conflict between a business or managerial need and a demonstrable educational need, the educational need should have priority. It is the burden of this first postulate that such conflicts are unlikely, if not impossible.

A second broad principle is that effective education demands administrative officers with the ability and willingness to think deeply about education and the forcefulness to act even in unpopular ways. There has grown up a theory of administration that places the initiative for change in the hands of the faculty. Administrative officers have frequently considered themselves more as board chairmen than as executive officers. This has resulted all too frequently in an aimless drift of the educational program. There is need in colleges for administrative officers who can earn the respect of faculty members by charting a course for the institution, mobilizing the energies of the faculty in that direction, and making the requisite decisions to achieve it. It is possible that compromise to accommodate the varying points of view of a faculty is not always the wisest administrative policy. Effective collegiate administration frequently demands that the administrative officer reach a decision which may, at the time taken, receive only limited and even grudging faculty support.

The last broad postulate is almost a generalized theory of collegiate administration. It holds that faculty members are essentially conservative. Many of them through work in their own subjects place great value on the past and on traditional ways of doing things. The very act of transmitting the culture from one generation to the next, which is an important part of the college professor's work, is a conservative act. The study of history, of political theory, or even of the classical sciences, signalizes a desire to value and to conserve the past. This attitude is carried over into faculty effort on educational matters. The caricature of the retiring professor, who remarked in faculty meeting that in his forty years at the institution he had witnessed many changes and had been against all of them, is not overdrawn.

Administrative officers in American society are agents of social change. They are the individuals who are constantly seeking new ways of doing things rather than conserving old ones. They are specifically charged with injecting new notions into the thinking of faculty members in the hope that change will take place. The administrative officer is the one who must find new experiences into which he can place recalcitrant faculty members so that the faculty member does change his behavior. In a way, the administrative officer should be as upsetting to the tranquillity of the faculty member as a teacher is to the established beliefs of his students.

If the destinies of an institution were left completely in the hands of faculty members, it is doubtful that much change would take place other than the gradual sort some anthropologists have recorded for primitive society. On the other hand, if the destinies of the institution were left exclusively in the hands of administrative

officers dedicated to change, the institutions over which they pre-
sided would be in such constant flux as to prevent any real educational progress. What is needed is a continuous tension between
the conservatism of the faculty and the dynamism of the administration, out of which healthy progress can be made. Out of the
sometimes sharp conflicts of administrative officers suggesting many
new ways of teaching, counseling, or organizing the curriculum,
and the faculty desire to perpetuate old ones, can come ways which
will really improve the entire process of education. It is from the
happy balance between strong-willed, capable administrative officers
and equally strong-willed and resilient faculty that effective administration for the small liberal arts college must come.

CHAPTER VI

Finances: Ever-Present Problem

Contemporary folkways have it that the characteristic salute of the American college president is one arm outstretched horizontally with palm turned up as he searches for the resources to maintain his institution. Bring any group of college presidents together and their conversation invariably turns irresistibly to matters of finance. Both of these illustrate the significant role of finances in the collegiate enterprise and underscore the problems which all institutions face in this regard.

American institutions of higher learning have never been well supported financially. Professors have been underpaid, considering the length of time spent in preparation and in comparison with other learned professions. The physical plants of the vast majority of such institutions have seldom been maintained as well as the plants of major industries. Budgets of colleges and universities have rarely been adequate to support even basic programs, much less activities of value but not absolutely necessary. Virtually no institution of higher learning has been able to offer a product which was paid for completely by the consumer of that product, hence has always been in economic terms an inefficient enterprise; and these conditions may be expected to intensify in the several decades ahead.

The approximately 3,800,000 students enrolled in institutions of higher learning in the fall of 1961 will double within ten years. If the American ideology continues to evolve in its present direction of insisting that large numbers of young people receive college education, over 80 per cent of the age group may well be enrolled in institutions of higher learning. Colleges and universities will be called upon to build the requisite physical plants, employ the necessary faculty, and maintain the essential materials for this larger number with very likely a smaller proportionate amount of financial support. Thus all colleges and universities, state-supported as well as private, can expect several decades of serious financial stress.

The smaller liberal arts college will face all the financial problems of its sister institutions, plus some of its own inherent ones. The liberal arts college, ranging from 250 to 1000 students, is typically too small to allow efficient management. If it attempts to offer a broad curriculum in the liberal arts and sciences it is almost forced to maintain costly classes for handfuls of students, particularly in the third and fourth years. If it is a residential institution, the numbers of students to be fed and housed are too small to allow the savings which come from large-scale purchasing operations. However small the number of its students, every institution must maintain certain essential administrative functions. The cost of these in large institutions becomes modest in terms of the large number of students paying tuition and being served, but it becomes excessive proportionately in smaller enterprises, simply because it must be prorated among such few students. Besides, since the smaller institutions obviously produce only a few graduates each year, the best of ultimate alumni support can never be very large. And if the institution happens to be one devoted to preparation for the service professions, it is unlikely that few, if any, extremely wealthy graduates will be produced.

A second related problem is that the majority of smaller institutions do not possess sufficient endowment to insure a steady basic income for their operation. The plight of these colleges may be compared with that of several of the more affluent ones which can afford to operate each year on the previous year's income from endowment and investments. The normal pattern for the small college is to operate on its current income from investments, its current tuitions, and its currently solicited gifts during the academic year. It is by no means rare for such institutions to have recourse to the banks in July of each year to obtain the necessary dollars to repair the physical plant, maintain salaries of the few 12-month appointees, and acquire the necessary supplies for the beginning of school the following year. The bank notes are retired with the first tuition money paid in. This hand-to-mouth existence has converted the small college president into a modern-day mendicant, who has little time for educational leadership, for staff recruiting, or for participation in the scholarly life.

Because the entire professional staff of the smaller liberal arts college is small, the institution can rarely afford to employ experienced and trained personnel to manage the finances and investments of the institution. While, as has been indicated in Chapter V, most colleges maintain a business manager or a comptroller, he must devote his energies to managing the physical plant and maintaining at least partially adequate bookkeeping procedures, looking out for long-term financing only with a small part of his attention. This situation may be contrasted with that at the University of Chicago, where ten full-time investment officers are maintained to insure that the support of the university rests on the highest possible yield from investments and supporting enterprises. While this is a little above average, the point is that the larger institutions are able to get adequate advice and assistance in their financial concerns, while the small ones are not.

Some of the financial problems of smaller institutions come from the fact that they are quite old and were founded in areas which have not become economically flourishing. Physical plants have not been maintained, partly because of sheer lack of funds and partly because of inadequate budgeting for depreciation. Yet such institutions are in competition with state institutions, many of which since World War II have created attractive new buildings to the extent that their campuses are almost completely new. Further, the locations of many of these small institutions have become cultural cul-de-sacs since the date of their origin. Thus situated, the institutions have not been able to attract students in sufficient numbers nor of sufficient ability.

Related to the sometimes undesirable location, obsolete physical plant, and inadequately trained faculty is the fact that many of the smaller liberal arts colleges have felt constrained to offer a disproportionate number of scholarships simply to attract the students needed to fill dormitories and classrooms. At the same time they have found it necessary to raise tuition in order to maintain even a semblance of competition with state-supported institutions. Since small schools normally derive about 60 per cent of their operating budgets from tuitions, these two procedures have resulted in a never-ending financial crisis. The higher tuition gave the low-tuition, state-supported institutions a competitive advantage, which the small college tried to offset by offering more scholarships. One can speculate that the net effect of this process has been a net loss in the revenue available, thus making solicitation of gift support even more imperative. While some schools have raised fees and increased the student body without added scholarships, only the well-known ones are safe in this regard.

Another major problem of the smaller liberal arts college is the reverse side of the aphorism that it takes money to make money. These frequently weaker institutions have not been able to attract the faculty members who would in turn attract major grants of money. They not infrequently have been unable to qualify for matching proportions made by major foundations or large donors. This point was dramatized when the Ford Foundation made its spectacular gift for faculty salaries. As a criterion to receive a grant it used accreditation by the regional accrediting association. This resulted in failure by perhaps the most needy of the smaller liberal arts colleges to receive any help for faculty salaries. The most recent Ford Foundation grant to privately supported liberal arts colleges went to eight of the strongest institutions in the nation. The more nearly average college, so frequently overlooked when large gifts and grants are being distributed, is with every failure to receive support in that much weaker position for the next turn of the spiral.

Still another perplexing problem of the smaller liberal arts college is the absence of adequate financial reserves to invest in personnel or devices which could ultimately result in substantial educational savings. By now it is axiomatic that much effective instruction can be carried on by closed-circuit television, but the equipment is beyond the resources of most liberal arts colleges. The addition of a psychiatrically trained counselor might result in curtailing an institution's high drop-out rate, yet this is a "frill" impossible for these schools to obtain. Within recent years there has been evidence that complete renovation of buildings, carpeting of classrooms, and other physical changes can enhance learning, yet the small institutions with seriously restricted budgets cannot hope to make these needed improvements.

The burden of all these specific problems is that the small privately supported liberal arts college typically does not have the necessary financial resources to carry out its minimal educational mission. Further, the inflationary spiral in which the society currently finds itself and the competition of tax supported, two-year and four-year institutions aggravate the condition year by year. While the financial plight of a number of such institutions is difficult

—and for a good many, serious—there are some palliatives which all might apply.

The first of these is to engage in more accurate budgeting and eventual cost accounting of both educational and other expenses. Although the publication of the American Council on Education, *College and University Business Administration,* has provided leadership for better budgetary procedures, a large number of the smaller institutions still do not follow the methods suggested. Budgeting too frequently consists of paying bills as long as money is available and then borrowing money until more tuition or gift money comes in, or budgeting optimistically on the basis of expected gifts and thus overcommitting the institution. For example, several years ago a patron of a small liberal arts college deeded to it several oil drillings. In view of past performance in the field, it was expected that an income of about half a million dollars a year would be realized. The institution budgeted on the strength of this expectation and employed staff on the basis of hopes, none of which were realized. The budgeting procedure should be as precise and realistic as men can make it and, further, an adequate system of budgetary control should be enforced so that units within the college live within their budgeted money. In addition to this form of accounting, the institutions might well study the cost of offering various programs. Reference has been made to the wide variation in cost of instruction between one subject and another. Once these figures are known, it is possible to make marked savings that can be used for other essential purposes. As more and more privately supported institutions make cost studies of instructional expenses, normative data are becoming available against which any institution can compare its own experience. The work of Russell and Doi, *Manual for Space Utilization in Colleges and Universities,* suggests ways to go about this problem.

A second palliative is for institutions to engage in more efficient fund-raising, including the cooperative ventures now characterizing some liberal arts colleges in a number of states. The very fact that corporate giving to privately-supported collegiate institutions has increased from nothing to its present levels is at least partly attributable to the efforts of statewide cooperative efforts of private institutions. According to the agreement, the presidents from all institutions contribute a certain amount of time each year to interviewing prospective large donors. The net gains from these efforts are distributed proportionately to the institutions engaging in the venture.

In addition to cooperative effort, the smaller institutions can make use of some of the growing number of consultant firms to help plan and carry out a development program. The best of these, having long years of experience, can advise an institution of the financial potential in a given constituency and the approximate cost of securing the funds it needs. Since a small institution cannot afford its own financial officers, wise use of consultants may help meet this perplexing problem. Parenthetically, smaller institutions may make use of other kinds of continuing consultations with equal value, such as obtaining the part-time services of a director of research employed in a larger institution. The half loaf may be better than none.

A third remedy is to move toward a more efficient operation of the entire educational program. Repeatedly throughout this book, the point has been made that the liberal arts curriculum is an expensive and wasteful effort. While older institutions may experience considerable difficulty in putting into effect completely the strictures suggested by Ruml and Morrison, at least the principles can be adapted. In their *Memo to a College Trustee* they show that by a judicious blending of large lecture courses, lecture discussion courses, and seminar tutorial courses, an adequate curriculum is possible, which will also allow adequate salaries for the teachers who conduct these. They argue that an institution of 800 students charging a tuition of $800 could pay salaries ranging from $7,000 to $18,000 a year after allowing for retirement and insurance deductions and reserves for sabbatical leaves. Such a possibility rests on offering eight large lecture courses, 32 lecture discussion courses, and 200 seminar tutorial courses. They maintain that for a school of this size to offer more courses is wasteful of resources and probably not productive of good education.

Along with a more efficient organization of the curriculum is the possibility of utilizing more efficient methods of teaching. The savings which can come from independent study, programmed learning, teacherless groups, and the like may have tremendous significance ultimately. And this is not simply speculating. One institution in 1961 abolished the sections in women's physical education, replacing them with a closed-circuit televised lesson which the students took in their rooms before the start of the day's classes. Institutions have always relied on students to teach one another a great many things, including foreign languages. One institution, for example, runs its elementary language sections with seniors who have spent a junior year studying in France.

A fourth device may be more difficult to put into effect, yet it must be recommended. Unless a private liberal arts college has considerable endowment, it cannot afford to operate a program for too small a number of students. There is probably some point— variously stated as 800 or 1000 students—below which diminishing returns set in. Institutions below that might well seek to move to such a level within a resonable time. Once an efficient-sized student body has been obtained, a number of other remedies to the financial condition become more possible.

Traditionally college fiscal officers have been extremely unimaginative and conservative in their administration of endowment funds. In part this is caused by a belief in a moral obligation to invest gift monies in only the most secure bonds, preferred stocks, and stable real estate. In part it is also related to the fact that college fiscal officers have had neither the time nor the knowledge to invest in more productive enterprises. It may be argued, however, that with the advice of capable members of boards of trustees, smaller colleges can put at least some of their reserve funds to earning substantially larger return than they now derive from blue chip securities.

The small, privately supported liberal arts college very likely must face up to constant increases in fees. This admittedly endangers such colleges by virtue of competition with low tuition, tax supported institutions. Increases in fees, however, can be so interpreted to patrons and to the public as to put them in a proper perspective. This point is made cogently by Howard R. Bowen in "Where Are the Dollars for Higher Education Coming From?", *Current Issues in Higher Education,* 1960, who says:

> First, I think the issue is less grave than usually supposed because too much attention is focused on tuition, which is only a fraction of the total cost of attending college. The true cost of attending college (as the economist would figure it) is the loss of income because the student forsakes employment and adds tuition and fees, transportation, books and supplies. I omit board, room, clothing and general

living expenses because the student would have these costs even if
he were working. Assuming conservatively that the average student
could earn $2500 a year if he were employed instead of studying,
the cost of four years of college, in terms of income forsaken, is
$10,000. Add to this an allowance for transportation, books and
supplies and the total cost without tuition becomes perhaps $11,000.
If he goes to a state institution with tuition and fees of $200 a year,
the total cost for four years is about $12,000. If he goes to an ex-
pensive private institution with tuitions and fees of $1000 a year,
the total cost becomes $15,000. The true cost of attending the ex-
pensive private institution is thus only about 25 per cent higher than
at the public institution, though the private tuition is five times the
public tuition.

Allied with this more appropriate interpretation of increase in
fees should come a realistic relating of fees to scholarship monies.
In 1958, Bennington College increased its fees substantially but at
the same time announced a policy of graduated scholarship grants
based on need. All entering students were required to pay the basic
cost of board and room. Those able to do so were required to pay
the full tuition on top of this. Students less able paid varying
amounts from no tuition above basic board and room costs to 90
per cent of full tuition. The plan was announced well in advance,
discussed thoroughly with students and communicated to their
parents, and apparently was well accepted. The increase in tuition
enabled the institution to increase faculty salaries as well as provide
even more scholarship money than it had in the past.

Better and more imaginative use of available space is still another
remedy open to the smaller liberal arts college. Some years ago, a
study of the available space in Illinois revealed that there was room
for 15,000 to 20,000 additional students if the existing space in
institutions of higher learning were better utilized. The currently
popular space utilization studies will show the way by which some
reforms can be made. Using classrooms throughout the day instead
of concentrating on the prime morning and early afternoon hours
may save dollars which normally would be put into new construction so that they can be used for increases in faculty salaries. As
important is imaginative use of space. With the Topsy-like growth
which has characterized so many of America's colleges, there are
corners and even major portions of campuses which are not used by
students simply because they are not attractive or seem off the

beaten path. One institution found its campus divided by a main traffic artery. Over the years one side of the road became the more desirable side and students could be placed on the other side only with difficulty and some drop in morale. Refurbishing the undesirable side and placing several highly popular activities there counteracted this swing, so that within two years the full sweep of the campus was available for fuller utilization.

While the use of space needs to be improved and can result in major savings, a word should perhaps be uttered regarding the presently popular trimester scheme. Within the past year a number of small liberal arts colleges have advanced plans for offering a trimester program. By and large these do not appear to have been successful. The American tradition of attending college for nine months with three months vacation is firmly embedded and one can argue that such a scheme is probably wise educationally. Education needs to be a leisurely matter. The student needs time to think about the ideas he has accumulated so that they become part of his intellectual resources. The long summer is possibly ideal for this. Further, it can be argued that faculties do need long periods of uninterrupted study if they are going to be thoroughly conversant with the subjects they profess. Part of the pressure on these smaller institutions to move to a trimester plan has come from faculties wanting and needing summer employment. If, however, some of the other economies have been put into effect, it is conceivable that salaries can be raised to a level making summer employment unnecessary. Thus faculty members can again find time for the scholarly life.

Since the history-making Ford Foundation grant for increase in funds for faculty salaries, the importance of accreditation in the financial affairs of a college has been recognized. Prospective donors want to insure that the institutions they support are sound and will do educational tasks adequately. Accreditation seems the only way currently available to insure the public of the soundness of institutions of higher learning. Thus unaccredited institutions are exerting every effort to gain this recognition. It is unfortunate that some of the weaker institutions have been persuaded that more effective public relations is the way by which accreditation could come, rather than by solid improvement. Any institution needs to interpret itself to its constituency and to the larger public, but it can interpret itself as strong only if it is in fact strong. The institution which seeks to sell itself as truly one of higher learning by means of an overly active public relations department does neither itself nor the cause of higher education much good.

A last suggested remedy involves greater cooperative effort with sister institutions in the same region. At a time when scientists and mathematicians are in scarce supply, liberal arts colleges located relatively near each other could very well offer joint appointments and thus meet the competition of the more affluent institutions. Judicious use of highly trained persons in nearby industry or in the professions is a similar method. The cooperative acquisition of library materials is still another. Perhaps nothing is quite such a drain on the privately supported liberal arts college as the music department. In a Southern boarder state are three liberal arts colleges within twenty-five miles of each other, each operating on a most modest budget and each with approximately thirty faculty members; yet each has a music department of six to ten teachers offering conservatory-type curriculums. The long-term health of all three and the educational needs of the region would be well served by some cooperative agreement under which one of the institutions would offer the music while the remaining two would offer other desirable programs. Institutions of higher learning have found that cooperative fund raising can work, that cooperative library holdings are possible; cooperative teaching ventures, cooperative purchasing, and cooperative programming are distinct possibilities.

Many other specific suggestions could be made. Since this is not a work primarily concerned with college finance, those presented may suffice to indicate the types of remedies available. It is appropriate, however, to suggest several broad financial considerations more far-reaching than those thus far suggested.

The first of these is to consider the possibility that at least some four-year, privately-supported liberal arts colleges should recognize officially that they are in fact two-year institutions. The attrition rate in many of these institutions is enormously high, ranging from 50 to 80 per cent, the large majority of students dropping out at the end of the second year. Large amounts of the resources of the institution are poured into offering upper level courses (and doing so inadequately), which could be used to provide a truly strong freshman and sophomore curriculum. Such a decision requires considerable knowledge on the part of the administration and certainly will run into obstacles of militant alumni groups. It may be that for some institutions this radical surgery is imperative, but two-year institutions pose unique problems. In view of the American ideology which holds that a college education is four years, unless a two-year institution offers a truly unique program or is located in a major population center it is likely to be unable to compete with tax-supported junior colleges or four-year institutions. It may be wise, therefore, for some liberal arts colleges converting to two-year institutions at the same time to move their location to areas of greater population density. In Chapter I an example of one institution which did move was presented. Several other colleges have made similar long-distance moves with a result of considerable strengthening of the entire enterprise.

As institutions consider such radical surgery, some might well face honestly the need to close their doors. These privately supported liberal arts colleges have been notoriously long-lived, but one must wonder whether or not some of them should continue to be encouraged to live. It is probably no real benefit to the society, nor to the students who attend, for an institution to exist in such a precarious financial condition that only the least able faculty members can be attracted. It is probably not conducive to a sound collegiate education for an institution to be so impoverished that the campus is unkempt, the buildings run down, and the equipment ill-maintained. Institutions with low resources might well discuss with capable counsel whether or not a closing of doors would be wise.

A second major reform has already been stressed in previous chapters, yet is so central as to demand restatement. This is for the privately supported liberal arts college to re-assert a primary purpose and then ruthlessly to delete all parts of the program which do not clearly contribute to it. It can be argued that if the fundamental purpose of a liberal arts college is still valid in American society, students will continue to attend, and that if it is not valid, this is bound to be reflected in the enrollments of the institution. To maintain enrollments by offering proliferal programs that could be as well offered in the large institutions is to fail to see the relevancy of the present situation.

Another major and certainly controversial suggestion is that the privately supported liberal arts colleges as well as the American society generally must reconsider the possibility of public support for such institutions. Actually, almost all the privately supported institutions have received governmental support at various times in their histories. Mighty Harvard was helped out of several precarious times by grants from the Commonwealth of Massachusetts. Kings College, later to be called Columbia, also received governmental subsidy. At present such a school as Ohio Wesleyan University has received a kind of federal subsidy in the form of reserve officer training corps units. The schools have all profited from federal grants indirectly through tax exemption and the tuitions provided by the several bills for the education of veterans. Federal research grants, and aid under the National Education Defense Act and through the College Housing Act have all assisted privately supported institutions. It perhaps is time, in view of the large numbers of young people who must be educated in the decades ahead, for the privately supported institutions to approach seriously the matter of securing either federal or state money. It may be that the New York State formula of straight tuition grants to students is the way. It is at least possible for tax monies to be paid directly to private institutions without jeopardizing the essential freedom which these colleges so prize. This will not come easily, but the experience of tax monies for the distinguished English institutions of Oxford and Cambridge suggest a model which American society might follow.

A last major revision is carrying to the logical conclusion a point made earlier. Privately supported institutions should raise their tuition fees to some workable level. If, after raising fees to a point at which an adequate budget is possible, the institution cannot attract sufficient students for economic operation, perhaps this should be taken as prima facie evidence that the institution should be closed. This point may sound harshly materialistic and economic. It is advanced out of the firm conviction that there is something wrong, if not outright fraudulent, about some small privately supported institutions' maintaining low tuitions, excessive scholarship grants, and ineffective educational plants simply to remain in operation. The point has been argued repeatedly through this book that the privately supported liberal arts college has a place in the American scene, but it has a place only when it is strong enough to provide an adequate program. An adequate program requires sound financing and efficient operation just as much as it does dedicated teaching. With the help of currently available knowledge, the small privately supported institution should decide what is a realistic budget in order to offer a first-rate education and what number of students is required to provide a vibrant intellectual climate and an efficient operation, and should take steps necessary to achieve these. Failure to do so within a reasonable time should perhaps be taken as a "mandate from heaven" for the institution to pass the torch to other and stronger hands.

Bibliography

Brubacher, John S. and Willis Rudy, *Higher Education in Translation*. New York: Harper & Brothers, 1958.

Brumbaugh, Aaron J., *Problems in College Administration*. Nashville, Tenn.: Abingdon Press, 1956.

Butts, R. Freeman, and Lawrence A. Cremin, *A History of Education in American Culture*. New York: Holt, Rinehart & Winston, Inc., 1953.

Cooper, Russell M., *Better Colleges—Better Teachers*. New York: The Macmillan Co., 1944.

Cowley, William H., *An Appraisal of American Higher Education*. Stanford, Calif.: Stanford University Press, 1956.

Cunningham, William F., *General Education and the Liberal College*. St. Louis, Mo.: Herder Book Company, 1953.

DeVane, William Clyde, *The American University in the Twentieth Century*. Baton Rouge, La.: Louisiana State University Press, 1957.

Earnest, Ernest, *Academic Procession: An Informal History of the American College*. New York: The Bobbs-Merrill Company, Inc., 1953.

Ficken, Clarence E., *Building a Faculty in a Church-Related College of Liberal Arts*. Nashville, Tenn.: Abingdon Press, 1956.

Gould, Samuel B., *Knowledge Is Not Enough*. Yellow Springs, Ohio: Antioch Press, 1959.

Griswold, Alfred W., *Liberal Education and the Democratic Ideal and Other Essays*. New Haven, Conn.: Yale University Press, 1959.

Harris, Seymour E., ed., *Higher Education in the United States: The Economic Problems*. Cambridge, Mass.: Harvard University Press, 1960.

Henderson, Algo D., *Policies and Practices in Higher Education*. New York: Harper & Brothers, 1960.

Hill, Alfred T., *The Small College Meets the Challenge*. New York: McGraw-Hill Book Company, Inc., 1959.

Hofstadter, Richard, and C. DeWitt Hardy, *The Development and Scope of Higher Education in the United States*. New York: Columbia University Press, 1952.

Hong, Howard, ed., *Integration in the Christian Liberal Arts College*. Northfield, Minn.: St. Olaf College, 1956.

Jacob, Phillip E., *Changing Values in College; An Exploratory Study of the Impact of College Teaching*. New York: Harper & Brothers, 1957.

Keezer, D. M., ed., *Financing Higher Education: 1960–1970*. New York: McGraw-Hill Book Company, Inc., 1959.

Knapp, Robert H., and Joseph Greenbaum, *The Younger American Scholar: His Collegiate Origins*. Chicago: University of Chicago Press, 1953.

Mayhew, Lewis B., ed., *General Education: An Account and Appraisal: A Guide for College Faculties*. New York: Harper & Brothers, 1960.

McGrath, Earl J., *Memo to a College Faculty Member*. New York: Columbia University Press, 1961.

McGrath, Earl J., and Charles H. Russell, *Are Liberal Arts Colleges Becoming Professional Schools?* New York: Bureau of Publications, Teachers College, Columbia University, 1958.

Mueller, Kate Hevner, *Student Personnel Work in Higher Education*. Boston: Houghton Mifflin Co., 1961.

Murphy, Lois B., and Esther Raushenbush, eds., *Achievement in the College Years*. New York: Harper & Brothers, 1960.

Riesman, David, *Constraint and Variety in American Education*. Lincoln, Neb.: University of Nebraska Press, 1956.

Russell, John Dale, *The Finance of Higher Education*, rev. ed. Chicago: University of Chicago Press, 1954.

Russell, John Dale, and James I. Doi, *Manual for Studies of Space Utilization in Colleges and Universities*. Washington, D.C.: American Council on Education, 1957.

Schmidt, George Paul, *The Liberal Arts College: A Chapter in American Cultural History*. New Brunswick, N.J.: Rutgers University Press, 1957.

Selden, William K., *Accreditation: A Struggle Over Standards in Higher Education*. New York: Harper & Brothers, 1960.

Stoke, Harold W., *The American College President*. New York: Harper & Brothers, 1959.

Tead, Ordway, *Trustees, Teachers, Students: Their Role in Higher Education*. Salt Lake City, Utah: University of Utah, 1951.

————, *The Climate of Learning*. New York: Harper & Brothers, 1958.

Trueblood, Elton, *The Idea of a College*. New York: Harper & Brothers, 1959.

Woodburne, Lloyd D., *Principles of College and University Administration*. Stanford, Calif.: Stanford University Press, 1958.

Index

Index

A

Academic freedom, 88
Accounting:
  procedures, 89
  for students, 75
Accreditation:
  agencies, 41, 42
  and finances, 101
Administration:
  continuity of, 80
  dynamism of officers, 91
  and educational theory, 90
  and leadership, 47, 80
  of student personnel, 73
Admission of students, 56, 78
Adult contact, 70 (*see also* Student)
Advising, 62
Alumni affairs, 64, 78
Automation (*see* Personnel services)

B

Birth rate, upsurge of, 8
Board of Control, 85
  duties, 87
Budget:
  analysis and control, 48, 97
Business management and educational
  effectiveness, 89

C

Catalogues, 38
Centralization of American life, 13
Competition for students, 15
Comptroller, 77
Consultant, 78, 98
Cooperative ventures, 97
Counseling, 62
Courses:
  multiplicity, 36
  number, 51
Cultural lag, 43
Curriculum:
  in colonial America, 36
  excessive expenses of, 98
  integration of, 39
  and personnel resources, 39
  and student personnel, 67

D

Dean of faculty, 75
  relationship with president, 86
Department head, 79
Departmental organization, 45
Departments, small, 15
Development officer, 77
Division head, 79
Drop-outs, 32

E

Economic benefits, 33
Education in flux, 48
Educational experiences, varieties of, 51
Elite, nurture of, 13
Employment (*see* Student)
Endowment, 94
Enrollments:
  college purpose, 15
  expanded, 7
  small, 15
Extra-curricular affairs, 65

F

Faculty:
  altruism, 19
  composition, 29
  conflicts with administration, 84
  financial condition of, 31
  financial plight, 22, 28
  and inheritances, 27
  participation in administration, 88
  part-time, 25
  physical examinations for, 33
  role, 9
Fads, 44
Fees:
  increases in, 99
  and scholarships, 100
Finances:
  conservatism of fiscal officers, 99
  financial reserves, 96
  and presidents, 93
  support, 93
Fraternity systems, 59
Fund-raising, 97

G

Geographic locations of colleges, 14, 95
General education, 38, 44
  purposes of undergraduate education, 50
Graduate education and liberal arts prerequisites, 52
Graduate schools:
  competition with, 37
  and liberal arts prerequisites, 52
  requirements, 46
  preparation for misguided, 58

H

Health (*see* Student)
Higher education:
  problems, 7
  and purposes, 7
  role, 8
Housing (*see* Student)

I

Institutional self-study, 47
Integration, arbitrary methods for, 49
Intellect, growth of a primary purpose, 9
Intellectual activity:
  centers of, 28, 35
  cul de sac, 29
  isolation of faculty, 35
Investments, management of, 94 (*see also* Finances)

K

Knowledge:
  increases in and the curriculum, 40
  proliferation of, 14
  variety of approaches, 51

L

Land-grant colleges, 40
Leadership:
  administrative, 47, 80
  educational, 79
Liberal arts colleges:
  American character of, 6
  characteristics, 1, 73
  disappearance of, 1
  emerging needs, 81
  private control, 5
  purposes, 5, 103
  size, 5
    efficiency and size, 99

Liberal arts colleges (*cont.*)
  support, 31
Liberal tradition and vocationalism, 12
Libraries, 22
  budget, 28
  librarian, 79
  vocational, 58

M

Majors:
  full coverage for, 43
  unnecessary, 32
Managerial techniques, 32
  efficiency, 94
Medical care, 63
Mental health, 64
Minority group status of small colleges, 16
Music departments, 37

O

Out-of-class life, 54

P

Part-time faculty, 25 (*see also* Faculty)
Personal problems, 63
Personnel services, 54, 76
  automation, 70
  staffing, 55, 67, 71
    competition for workers, 71
    motivations of student personnel workers, 71
  theory of, 55, 68
Ph.D's:
  earned, 24
  proportion of, 23
Placement, 59
President:
  duties, 83
  and finance, 93
  relationship with dean, 82, 86
Primary groups (*see* Student)
Projection as defense, 22
Professional growth, 33
Professors:
  average, 17
  characteristics, 18
  differences, 18
  marginality, 20
  and society, 18
  view their profession, 19
  (*see also* Faculty)
Programmed learning, 71
Programs, high cost, 31

Proliferation, reasons for, 37
Public relations, 78
Public support for private colleges, 104
Publication, 34

R

Reality and expectation, conflict between, 20
Record keeping, 72
Recruitment (*see* Students)
Regional cooperation, 34
Registrar, 75
Religious life, 62
Residence halls, 59
Ruml report, 40

S

Salaries, limited, 25
Scholarship and curriculum, 44 (*see also* Curriculum)
Scholarships:
  and financial aid, 64
  number, 95
Secularism and Christian religion, 11
Shared responsibility, 84
Small colleges, peculiar problems of, 10
Social life, 61
Society, emerging needs, 49
Space utilization, 100
Staffs:
  administrative structure, 74
  finding and maintaining, 9
Students:
  admission, 56, 78
  and career decisions, 58
  collection of information, 72
  employment, 64
  government, 60
  health, 63
  housing, 59
  life, 61
    changing pattern of, 61
  needs, 69, 70
  numbers, 93

Students (*cont.*)
  orientation of student affairs, 57
  orientation of, 67
  and primary groups, 69
  recruitment, 56
  regulation of behavior, 66
  and support, 65

T

Teaching:
  and curriculum, 21
  improvement of, 34
  and heavy loads, 21
  problems of, 21
  and unrelated fields, 24
Teachers:
  preparation, 23, 30
  scholarly life of, 26
  (*see also* Faculty)
Termination of weak colleges, 103
Testing, 57
Theoretical structure for curricula, 50
Transportation, 28
Treasurer, 77
Tri-mester, 101
Tuition:
  increases in, 104
  and salaries, 31
Two-year college, 102

U

Units, academic, 81
Unity of liberal arts, 36
Universal education, 7

V

Value conflict, 11
Vocational libraries, 58 (*see also* Libraries)
Vocationalism, 41

W

Wheel analogy, 53